NILES PUBLIC LIBRARY

Niles, Illinois

FINE SCHEDULE

Adult Materials . . . . 10 per day
Juvenile Materials . . . . . . 04 per day
Video Tapes . . . . . . $1.50 per day

Modern Critical Interpretations

William Shakespeare's
Hamlet

Modern Critical Interpretations

These and other titles in preparation

Modern Critical Interpretations

William Shakespeare's
Hamlet

Edited and with an introduction by
Harold Bloom
Sterling Professor of the Humanities
Yale University

CHELSEA HOUSE PUBLISHERS ◊ 1986
NEW YORK ◊ NEW HAVEN ◊ PHILADELPHIA

Library of Congress Cataloging-in-Publicaton Data
    Main entry under title:
    William Shakespeare's Hamlet.
        (Modern critical interpretations)
        Bibliography: p.
        Includes index.
        Summary: A collection of eight critical essays on
    Shakespeare's play "Hamlet" arranged in chronological
    ordr of publication from 1951 to the present.
        1. Shakespeare, William, 1564–1616.   Hamlet — Ad-
    dresses, essays, lectures. [1. Shakespeare,
    William, 1564–1616.   Hamlet — Addresses, essays,
    lectures]   I. Bloom, Harold.   II. Series.
PR2807.W456   1986   822.3'3   85–29903
ISBN 0-87754-924-9

Contents

Editor's Note

This volume gathers together a selection of the most illuminating literary criticism devoted to *Hamlet* from 1951 to the present day, arranged in the chronological order of its publication. The editor is grateful to Marena Fisher for her assistance in choosing the eight essays that here explore the most famous and influential of all Shakespeare's dramas.

The editor's introduction engages the difficult issue of Shakespeare's originality as manifested by Hamlet's comprehensiveness as a representation. In particular, it attempts to understand the way in which Hamlet's character, by changing radically during the intervals between Acts IV and V, subsequently informs and gives coherence to an idea of disinterestedness that we could not know had Shakespeare not written the play.

Harold Goddard, in the editor's judgment the best modern critic of Shakespeare, begins the chronological sequence with an eloquent celebration of a Hamlet who "is his own Falstaff," who indeed is Falstaff's only rival as prince of wit in all the world's literature. Perhaps Goddard somewhat overidealizes Hamlet, but the next essay, Harry Levin's brilliant dialectical explication of the Player's speech, returns us to the trickier aspects of Shakespeare's rhetorical art, while reminding us of the tradition that Shakespeare himself played the ghost of Hamlet's father, and very possibly doubled as the First Player also.

Ruth Nevo, examining some of the problems of text and staging, particularly as they concern the integrity of Act IV, can be said to reidealize the hero, but in a more realistic mode than Goddard's. A darker vision is suggested by Lawrence Danson's analysis of tragic language in *Hamlet,* where the play's reliance upon acutely meaningful words and gestures is set against its dramatic context or cosmos in which words and gestures alike have lost all meaning. Closely related is the distinction perceptively worked through in Richard A. Lanham's essay, which is the difference between *playing* someone and *being* someone, a difference that I would judge not to be present in the Hamlet of Act V.

Howard Felperin analyzes *Hamlet* as Shakespeare's transformation of older forms, whether of the morality play, or the revenge tragedy of Kyd. Felperin's concentration on the modernity of Shakespearean mimesis is complemented by Mark Rose's exegesis of how the play reforms the hero's role of melodrama by purifying it of all vulgarity. The final essay, Francis Barker's Foucault-inspired study of "subjection" in *Hamlet,* depicts a cosmos "top-heavy with visibility," a kind of metaphysical realm of pure spectacle. To find that Shakespeare "contains" Foucault perhaps only tells us again that Hamlet's consciousness remains the largest and most comprehensive of all Western representations of human character and personality.

Introduction

The last we see of Hamlet at the court in Act IV is his exit for England:

HAMLET: For England?

CLAUDIUS: Ay, Hamlet.

HAMLET: Good.

CLAUDIUS: So is it, if thou knew'st our purposes.

HAMLET: I see a cherub that sees them. But come, for England! Farewell, dear mother.

CLAUDIUS: Thy loving father, Hamlet.

HAMLET: My mother: father and mother is man and wife, man and wife is one flesh — so my mother. Come, for England!

Exit

It is a critical commonplace to assert that the Hamlet of Act V is a changed man: mature rather than youthful, certainly quieter, if not quietistic, and somehow more attuned to divinity. Perhaps the truth is that he is at last himself, no longer afflicted by mourning and melancholia, by murderous jealousy and incessant rage. Certainly he is no longer haunted by his father's ghost. It may be that the desire for revenge is fading in him. In all of Act V he does not speak once of his dead father directly. There is a single reference to "my father's signet" which serves to seal up the doom of those poor schoolfellows, Rosencrantz and Guildenstern, and there is the curious phrasing of "my king" rather than "my father" in the halfhearted rhetorical question the prince addresses to Horatio:

> Does it not, think thee, stand me now upon—
> He that hath kill'd my king and whor'd my mother,
> Popp'd in between th'election and my hopes,
> Thrown out his angle for my proper life
> And with such coz'nage — is't not perfect conscience
> To quit him with this arm?

When Horatio responds that Claudius will hear shortly from England, presumably that Rosencrantz and Guildenstern have been executed, Hamlet rather ambiguously makes what might be read as a final vow of revenge:

> It will be short. The interim is mine.
> And a man's life's no more than to say "one."

However this is to be interpreted, Hamlet forms no plot, and is content with a wise passivity, knowing that Claudius must act. Except for the scheme of Claudius and Laertes, we and the prince might be confronted by a kind of endless standoff. What seems clear is that the urgency of the earlier Hamlet has gone. Instead, a mysterious and beautiful disinterestedness dominates this truer Hamlet, who compels a universal love precisely because he is beyond it, except for its exemplification by Horatio. What we overhear is an ethos so original that we still cannot assimilate it:

> Sir, in my heart there was a kind of fighting
> That would not let me sleep. Methought I lay
> Worse than the mutines in the bilboes. Rashly—
> And prais'd be rashness for it: let us know
> Our indiscretion sometimes serves us well
> When our deep plots do pall; and that should learn us
> There's a divinity that shapes our ends,
> Rough-hew them how we will—

Weakly read, that divinity is Jehovah, but more strongly "ends" here are not our intentions but rather our fates, and the contrast is between a force that can *shape* stone, and our wills that only hew roughly against implacable substance. Nor would a strong reading find Calvin in the echoes of the Gospel of Matthew as Hamlet sets aside his own: "Thou wouldst not think how ill all's here about my heart." In his heart, there is again a kind of fighting, but the readiness, rather than the ripeness, is now all:

> Not a whit. We defy augury. There is special providence in the fall of
> a sparrow. If it be now, 'tis not to come; if it be not to come, it will
> be now; if it be not now, yet it will come. The readiness is all. Since
> no man, of aught he leaves, knows aught, what is't to leave betimes?
> Let be.

The apparent nihilism more than negates the text cited from Matthew, yet the epistemological despair does not present itself as despair, but as an achieved serenity. Above all else, these are not the accents of an avenger, or even of someone who still mourns, or who continues to suffer the selfish virtues of the natural heart. Not nihilism but authentic disinterestedness, and yet what is that? No Elizabethan lore, no reading in Aristotle, or even in Montaigne, can help to answer that question. We know the ethos of disinterestedness only because we know Hamlet. Nor can we hope to know Hamlet any better by knowing Freud. The dead father indeed was, during four acts, more powerful than even the living one could be, but by Act V the dead father is not even a numinous shadow. He is merely a precursor, Hamlet the Dane before this one, and this one matters much more. The tragic hero in Shakespeare, at his most universally moving, is a representation so original that conceptually *he contains us,* and fashions our psychology of motives permanently. Our map or general theory of the mind may be Freud's, but Freud, like all the rest of us, inherits the representation of mind, at its most subtle and excellent, from Shakespeare. Freud could say that the aim of all life was death, but not that readiness is all.

II

Originality in regard to Shakespeare is a bewildering notion, because we have no rival to set him against. "The originals are not original," Emerson liked to remark, but he withdrew that observation in respect to Shakespeare. If Shakespeare had a direct precursor it had to be Marlowe, who was scarcely six months older. Yet, in comparison to Shakespeare, Marlowe represents persons only by caricature. The Chaucer who could give us the Pardoner or the Wife of Bath appears to be Shakespeare's only authentic English precursor, if we forget the English renderings of the Bible. Yet we do not take our psychology from Chaucer or even from the Bible. Like Freud himself, we owe our psychology to Shakespeare. Before Shakespeare, representations in literature may change *as* they speak, but they do not change *because* of what they say. Shakespearean representation turns upon his persons listening to themselves simultaneously with our listening, and learning and changing even as we learn and change. Falstaff delights himself as much as he delights us, and Hamlet modifies himself by studying his own modifications. Ever since, Falstaff has been the inescapable model for nearly all wit, and Hamlet the paradigm for all introspection. When Yorick's skull replaces the helmeted ghost, then the mature Hamlet has replaced the self-chastising revenger, and a different sense of death's power over life has been created, and in more than a play or a dramatic poem:

> HAMLET: To what base uses we may return, Horatio! Why may not
> imagination trace the noble dust of Alexander till a find it stop-
> ping a bunghole?
> HORATIO: 'Twere to consider too curiously to consider so.
> HAMLET: No, faith, not a jot, but to follow him thither with mod-
> esty enough, and likelihood to lead it.

Probability leads possibility, likelihood beckons imagination on, and Alexander is essentially a surrogate for the dead father, the Danish Alexander. Passionately reductive, Hamlet would consign his own dust to the same likelihood, but there we part from him, with Horatio as our own surrogate. Hamlet's unique praise of Horatio sets forever the paradigm of the Shakespearean reader or playgoer in relation to the Shakespearean tragic hero:

> Dost thou hear?
> Since my dear soul was mistress of her choice,
> And could of men distinguish her election,
> Sh'ath seal'd thee for herself; for thou hast been
> As one, in suff'ring all, that suffers nothing . . .

Which means, not that Horatio and the reader do not suffer with Hamlet, but rather that truly they suffer nothing precisely because they learn from Hamlet the disinterestedness they themselves cannot exemplify, though in possibility somehow share. And they survive, to tell Hamlet's story "of accidental judgments" not so accidental and perhaps not judgments, since disinterestedness does not judge, and there are no accidents.

Only Hamlet, at the last, is disinterested, since the hero we see in Act V, despite his protestations, is now beyond love, which is not to say that he never loved Gertrude, or Ophelia, or the dead father, or poor Yorick for that matter. Hamlet is an actor? Yes, earlier, but not in Act V, where he has ceased also to be a play director, and finally even abandons the profession of poet. Language, so dominant as such in the earlier Hamlet, gives almost the illusion of transparency in his last speech, if only because he verges upon saying what cannot be said:

> You that look pale and tremble at this chance,
> That are but mutes or audience to this act,
> Had I but time—as this fell sergeant, Death,
> Is strict in his arrest—O, I could tell you—
> But let it be.

Evidently he does know something of what he leaves, and we ache to know what he could tell us, since it is Shakespeare's power to persuade us that Hamlet has gained a crucial knowledge. One clue is the abiding theatrical trope of "but mutes or audience," which suggests that the knowledge is itself "of" illusion. But the trope is framed by two announcements to Horatio and so to us—"I am dead"—and no other figure in Shakespeare seems to stand so authoritatively on the threshold between the worlds of life and death. When the hero's last speech moves between "O, I die, Horatio" and "the rest is silence," there is a clear sense again that much more might be said, concerning our world and not the "undiscovered country" of death. The hint is that Hamlet could tell us something he has learned about the nature of representation, because he has learned what it is that he himself represents.

Shakespeare gives Fortinbras the last word on this, but that word is irony, since Fortinbras represents only the formula of repetition: like father, like son. "The soldier's music and the rite of war" speak loudly for the dead father, but not for this dead son, who had watched the army of Fortinbras march past to gain its little patch of ground and had mused that: "Rightly to be great / Is not to stir without great argument." The reader's last word has to be Horatio's, who more truly than Fortinbras has Hamlet's dying voice: "and from his mouth whose voice will draw on more," which only in a minor key means draw more supporters to the election of Fortinbras. Horatio represents the audience, while Fortinbras represents all the dead fathers.

III

We love Hamlet, then, for whatever reasons Horatio loves him. Of Horatio we know best that what distinguishes him from Rosencrantz and Guildenstern, and indeed from Polonius, Ophelia, Laertes, and Gertrude, is that Claudius *cannot use him*. Critics have remarked upon Horatio's ambiguously shifting status at the court of Denmark, and the late William Empson confessed a certain irritation at Hamlet's discovery of virtues in Horatio that the prince could not find in himself. Yet Shakespeare gives us a Hamlet we must love while knowing our inferiority, since he has the qualities we lack, and so he also gives us Horatio, our representative, who loves so stoically for the rest of us. Horatio is loyal, and limited; skeptical as befits a fellow student of the profoundly skeptical Hamlet, yet never skeptical about Hamlet. Take Horatio out of the play, and you take us out of the play. The plot could be rearranged to spare the wretched Rosencrantz and Guildenstern, even to spare Laertes, let alone Fortinbras, but remove Horatio, and Hamlet becomes so estranged from us that we scarcely can hope to account for that universality of appeal which is his, and the play's, most original characteristic.

Horatio, then, represents by way of our positive association with him; it is a commonplace, but not less true for that, to say that Hamlet represents by negation. I think this negation is Biblical in origin, which is why it seems so Freudian to us, because Freudian negation is Biblical and not Hegelian, as it were. Hamlet is Biblical rather than Homeric or Sophoclean. Like the Hebrew hero confronting Yahweh, Hamlet needs to be everything in himself yet knows the sense in which he is nothing in himself. What Hamlet takes back from repression is returned only cognitively, never affectively, so that in him thought is liberated from its sexual past, but at the high expense of a continued and augmenting sense of sexual disgust. And what Hamlet at first loves is what Biblical and Freudian man loves: the image of authority, the dead father, and the object of the dead father's love, who is also the object of Claudius' love. When Hamlet matures, or returns fully to himself, he transcends the love of authority, and ceases to love at all, and perhaps he can be said to be dying throughout all of Act V, and not just in the scene of the duel.

In Freud, we love authority, but authority does not love us in return. Nowhere in the play are we told, by Hamlet or by anyone else, of the love of the dead king for his son, but only for Gertrude. That Hamlet hovers always beyond our comprehension must be granted, yet he is not so far beyond as to cause us to see him with the vision of Fortinbras, rather than the vision of Horatio. We think of him not necessarily as royal, but more as noble, in the archaic sense of "noble" which is to be a seeing soul. It is surely no accident that Horatio is made to emphasize the word "noble" in his elegy for Hamlet, which contrasts angelic song to "the soldier's music" of Fortinbras. As a noble or seeing heart, Hamlet indeed sees feelingly. Short of T. S. Eliot's judgment that the play is an aesthetic failure, the oddest opinion in the *Hamlet* criticism of our time was that of W. H. Auden in his Ibsen essay, "Genius and Apostle," which contrasts Hamlet as a mere actor to Don Quixote as the antithesis of an actor:

> Hamlet lacks faith in God and in himself. Consequently he must define his existence in terms of others, e.g., I am the man whose mother married his uncle who murdered his father. He would like to become what the Greek tragic hero is, a creature of situation. Hence his inability to act, for he can only "act," i.e., play at possibilities.

Harold Goddard, whose *The Meaning of Shakespeare* (1951) seems to me still the most illuminating single book on Shakespeare, remarked that, "Hamlet is his own Falstaff." In Goddard's spirit, I might venture the formula that Brutus plus Falstaff equals Hamlet, though "equals" is hardly an accurate word here. A better formula was proposed by A. C. Bradley, when he suggested that Hamlet was the only Shakespearean character whom we could think had written Shakespeare's plays. Goddard built on this by saying of Shakespeare: "He is an unfallen Hamlet." From a scholarly or any Formalist perspective, Goddard's aphorism is not criticism, but neither historical research nor Formalist modes of criticism have helped us much in learning to describe the unassimilated originality that Shakespearean representation still constitutes. Because we are formed by Shakespeare, paradoxically most fully where we cannot assimilate him, we are a little blinded by what might be called the originality of this originality. Only a few critics (A. D. Nuttall among them) have seen that the central element in this originality is its cognitive power. Without Shakespeare (and the Bible as his precursor text) we would not know of a literary representation that worked so as to compel "reality" (be it Platonic or Humean, Hegelian or Freudian) to reveal aspects of itself we previously could not discern. Such a representation cannot be considered antimimetic or an effect of language alone.

IV

One way, by no means unproductive, of accounting for the force of Shakespearean representation is to see it as the supreme instance of what the late Paul de Man called a poetics of modernity, of a revisionism of older literary conventions that at once subsumed and cancelled the illusions always present in all figurative language. Howard Felperin, working in de Man's mode, adroitly reads Macbeth's "modernity" as the dilemma of a figure totally unable to take his own nature for granted: "He cannot quite rest content in an action in which his role and his nature are determined in advance, but must continuously reinvent himself in the process of acting them out." In such a view, Macbeth is a strong misreading of a figure like Herod in the old morality plays. I would go further and suggest that the drama *Macbeth* is an allusive triumph over more formidable precursors, just as *King Lear* is. The Shakespearean Sublime, too strong to find agonists in Seneca or in the native tradition (even in Marlowe), and too remote from Athenian drama to feel its force, confronts instead the Sublime of the Bible. What breaks loose in the apocalyptic cosmos of *Macbeth* or of *Lear* is an energy of the abyss or the original chaos that is ignored in the priestly first chapter of Genesis, but which wars fiercely against Jehovah in crucial passages of Job, the Psalms, and Isaiah. To subsume and supersede the Bible could not have been the conscious ambition of Shakespeare, but if we are to measure the preternatural energies of *Macbeth* or of *Lear*, then we will require Job or Isaiah or certain Psalms as the standard of measurement.

What is the advance, cognitive and figurative, that Shakespearean representation achieves over Biblical depiction? The question is absurdly difficult, yet anything but meaningless. If Shakespeare has a true Western rival, then he is either the Yahwist, the Hebrew Bible's great original, or the Homer of the *Iliad*. Can there *be* an advance over Jacob or Achilles as representations of reality, whatever that is taken to be? What the question reduces to is the unanswerable: can there be advances in reality? The arts, as Hazlitt insisted, are not progressive, and if reality is, then its progression suspiciously resembles a speeding up of what Freud called the death drive. Reality testing, like the reality principle, is Freud's only transcendentalism, his last vestige of Platonism. Freud's own originality, as he deeply sensed, tends to evaporate when brought too near either to the originality of the Yahwist or to the originality of Shakespeare. This may be the true cause of the disaster that is *Moses and Monotheism,* and of Freud's own passion for the lunatic thesis that Shakespeare's plays were written by the Earl of Oxford.

By Nietzsche's genealogical test for the memorable, which is cognitive pain,

Job is no more nor less forgettable than *Macbeth* or *Lear*. The rhetorical economy of Job's wife, in her one appearance, unmatchable even out of context, is overwhelming within context, and may have set for Shakespeare one of the limits of representation:

> So went Satan forth from the presence of the Lord, and smote Job with sore boils from the sole of his foot unto his crown.
>
> And he took him a potsherd to scrape himself withal; and he sat down among the ashes.
>
> Then said his wife unto him, Dost thou still retain thine integrity? Curse God, and die.

Lear's Queen, the mother of Goneril, Regan, and Cordelia, had she survived to accompany her husband onto the heath, hardly could have said more in less. In Shakespeare's tragedies there are moments of compressed urgency that represent uncanny yet persuasive change with Biblical economy. The dying Edmund sees the bodies of Goneril and Regan brought in, and belatedly turns his lifetime about in four words: "Yet Edmund was belov'd." The phrase is a vain attempt to countermand his own order for the murder of Cordelia. "Yet Edmund was belov'd"—though loved by two fiends, the shock of knowing he *was* loved, unto death, undoes "mine own nature." One thinks of Hamlet's "Let be" that concludes his "We defy augury" speech, as he goes into the trap of Claudius' last plot. "Let be" epitomizes what I have called "disinterestedness," though Horatio's word "noble" may be more apt. That laconic "Let be," repeated as "Let it be" in Hamlet's death speech, is itself a kind of catastrophe creation, even as it marks another phase in Hamlet's release from what Freud called the family romance, and even as it compels another transference for our veneration to Hamlet. Catastrophe creation, family romance, transference: these are the stigmata and consequently the paradigms for imaginative originality in the Bible and, greatly shadowed, in Freud, and I suggest now that they can be useful paradigms for the apprehension of originality in Shakespeare's tragic representations. The fantasy of rescuing the mother from degradation is palpable in Hamlet; less palpable and far more revelatory is the sense in which the prince has molded himself into a pragmatic changeling. The ghost is armed for war, and Hamlet, grappling with Laertes in the graveyard, accurately warns Laertes (being to that extent his father's son) that as the prince he has something dangerous in him. But is Hamlet psychically ever armed for war? Claudius, popping in between the election and Hamlet's hopes, could have shrewdly pled more than his nephew's youth and inexperience while properly arguing that his own nature was better qualified for the throne. Hamlet, in the graveyard, shocked back from beyond affect, accurately indicates whose true son he first became as changeling:

Alas, poor Yorick. I knew him, Horatio, a fellow of infinite jest, of most excellent fancy. He hath bore me on his back a thousand times, and now—how abhorred in my imagination it is. My gorge rises at it. Here hung those lips that I have kissed I know not how oft . . .

Harry Levin, for whom strong misreading is not serendipity but misfortune, advises us that "Hamlet without *Hamlet* has been thought about all too much." One might reply, in all mildness, that little memorable has been written about *Hamlet* that does not fall into the mode of "Hamlet without *Hamlet*." Far more even than *Lear* or *Macbeth,* the play is the figure; the question of *Hamlet* only can be Hamlet. He does not move in a Sublime cosmos, and truly has no world except himself, which would appear to be what he has learned in the interim between Acts IV and V. Changelings who move from fantasy to fact are possible only in romance, and alas Shakespeare wrote the tragedy of Hamlet, and not the romance of Hamlet instead. But the originality of Shakespearean representation in tragedy, and particularly in *Hamlet,* hardly can be overstressed. Shakespeare's version of the family romance always compounds it with two other paradigms for his exuberant originality: with a catastrophe that creates and with a carrying across from earlier ambivalences within the audience to an ambivalence that is a kind of taboo settling in about the tragic hero like an aura. At the close of *Hamlet,* only Horatio and Fortinbras are survivors. Fortinbras presumably will be another warrior-king of Denmark. Horatio does not go home with us, but vanishes into the aura of Hamlet's afterlight, perhaps to serve as witness of Hamlet's story over and over again. The hero leaves us with a sense that finally he has fathered himself, that he was beyond our touch though not beyond our affections, and that the catastrophes he helped provoke have brought about, not a new creation, but a fresh revelation of what was latent in reality but not evident without his own disaster.

V

As a coda, I return to my earlier implication that Shakespearean originality is the consequence of diction or a will over language changing his characters, and not of language itself. More than any other writer, Shakespeare is able to exemplify how meaning gets started rather than just renewed. Auden remarked that Falstaff is free of the superego; there is no over-I or above-I for that triumph of wit. Nietzsche, attempting to represent a man without a superego, gave us Zarathustra, a mixed achievement in himself, but a very poor representation when read side by side with Falstaff. Falstaff or Zarathustra? No conceivable reader would choose the Nietzschean rather than the Shakespearean over-man. Falstaff indeed *is* how meaning gets started: by excess, overflow, emanation, contamination, the will to life. Zarathustra is a juggler of perspectives, a receptive will to interpretation. Poor Falstaff ends in tragedy; his catastrophe is his dreadfully authentic love for Hal. Zarathustra loves only a trope, the solar trajectory, and essentially is himself a trope; he is Nietzsche's metalepsis or transumption of the philosophical tradition. A Formalist critic would say that Falstaff is a trope also, a gorgeous and glowing hyperbole. Say rather that Falstaff is a representation, in himself, of how meaning gets started, of how invention is accomplished and manifested. But we remember Falstaff as we want to remember him, triumphant in the tavern, and not rejected in the street. We remember Hamlet as he wanted us to remember him, as Horatio remembers him, without having to neglect his end. Perhaps Hamlet is a representation, in himself, not just of how meaning gets started, but also of how meaning itself is invention, of how meaning refuses to be deferred or to be ended. Perhaps again that is why we can imagine Hamlet as the author of *Hamlet*, as the original we call Shakespeare.

Hamlet: His Own Falstaff

Harold Goddard

To nearly everyone both Hamlet himself and the play give the impression of having some peculiarly intimate relation to their creator. What that relation may
originally have been we shall probably never know. But it is hard to refrain from
speculating. When we learn that Dostoevsky had a son, Alyosha (Alexey), whom
he loved dearly and who died before he was three, and that the father began
writing *The Brothers Karamazov* that same year, the temptation is irresistible to
believe that its hero, Alexey Karamazov, is an imaginative reincarnation of the
child, a portrayal of what the author would have liked the boy to become. In this
instance the father bestowed an immortality that there is only a negligible chance
the son would have achieved if he had lived. Shakespeare's son Hamnet died at
the age of eleven, possibly not long before his father began to be attracted by the
Hamlet story. Was there any connection? We do not know. But the name, in its
interchangeable forms, must have had strong emotional associations for Shakespeare. Hamnet and Judith Sadler, neighbors and friends of the Shakespeares,
were godparents to their twins, to whom they gave their names. When Shakespeare was sixteen, a girl, Katherine Hamlett, was drowned near Stratford under
circumstances the poet may have remembered when he told of Ophelia's death.
Resemblances between Hamlet and the Earl of Essex, who, in turn, figured significantly in Shakespeare's life, have frequently been pointed out.

However all this may be, there is no doubt that Shakespeare endowed
Hamlet with the best he had acquired up to the time he conceived him. He inherits the virtues of a score of his predecessors — and some of their weaknesses.

From *The Meaning of Shakespeare.* © 1951 by the The University of Chicago. The University of
Chicago Press, 1951. Originally entitled "Hamlet."

Yet he is no mere recapitulation of them. In him, rather, they recombine to make a man as individual as he is universal. He has the passion of Romeo ("Romeo is Hamlet in love," says Hazlitt), the dash and audacity of Hotspur, the tenderness and genius for friendship of Antonio, the wit, wisdom, resourcefulness, and historionic gift of Falstaff, the bravery of Faulconbridge, the boyish charm of the earlier Hal at his best, the poetic fancy of Richard II, the analogic power and meditative melancholy of Jaques, the idealism of Brutus, the simplicity and human sympathy of Henry VI, and, after the assumption of his antic disposition, the wiliness and talent for disguise of Henry IV and the cynicism and irony of Richard III—not to mention gifts and graces that stem more from certain of Shakespeare's heroines than from his heroes—for, like Rosalind, that inimitable boy-girl, Hamlet is an early draft of a new creature on the Platonic order, conceived in the *Upanishads,* who begins to synthesize the sexes. "He who understands the masculine and keeps to the feminine shall become the whole world's channel. Eternal virtue shall not depart from him and he shall return to the state of an infant." If Hamlet does not attain the consummation that Laotse thus describes, he at least gives promise of it. What wonder that actresses have played his role, or that among the theories about him one of the most inevitable, if most insane, is that he is a woman in disguise! Mad literally, the idea embodies a symbolic truth and helps explain why Hamlet has been pronounced both a hero and a dreamer, hard and soft, cruel and gentle, brutal and angelic, like a lion and like a dove. One by one these judgments are all wrong. Together they are all right—

> These contraries such unity do hold,

a line which those who object to such paradoxes as "modernizing" should note is Shakespeare's, as is also the phrase "mighty opposites."

For what was such a man made? Plainly for the ultimate things: for wonder, for curiosity and the pursuit of truth, for love, for creation—but first of all for freedom, the condition of the other four. He was made, that is, for religion and philosophy, for love and art, for liberty to "grow unto himself"—five forces that are the elemental enemies of Force.

And this man is called upon to kill. It is almost as if Jesus had been asked to play the role of Napoleon (as the temptation in the wilderness suggests that in some sense he was). If Jesus had been, ought he to have accepted it? The absurdity of the question prompts the recording of the strangest of all the strange facts in the history of *Hamlet:* the fact, namely, that nearly all readers, commentators, and critics are agreed in thinking that it was Hamlet's duty to kill, that he ought indeed to have killed much sooner than he did. His delay, they say, was a weakness and disaster, entailing, as it did, many unintended deaths, including his own. He should have obeyed much earlier the Ghost's injunction to avenge his father's murder. "Surely it is clear," says Bradley, giving expression to this idea for a multitude of others, "that, whatever we in the twentieth century may think about Hamlet's duty, we are meant in the play to assume that he *ought* to have obeyed the Ghost." "As for the morality of personal vengeance," says Hazelton Spencer, "however abhorrent the concept we must accept it in the play as Hamlet's sacred duty, just as we must accept the Ghost who urges it." "John-a-dreams tarried long," says Dover Wilson at the end of *What Happens in Hamlet*, "but this Hercules 'sweeps' to his revenge." And with plain approval he pronounces Hamlet's "task accomplished," his "duty now performed."

Now whatever we are "meant" to assume, there is no doubt that nearly every spectator and reader the first time he encounters the play does assume that Hamlet ought to kill the King — and nearly all continue in that opinion on further acquaintance in the face of the paradox just stated.

How can that be?

It can be for the same reason that we exult when Gratiano cries, "Now, infidel, I have thee on the hip," and we see Shylock get what he was about to give, for the same reason that we applaud when Romeo sends Tybalt to death, and are enthralled by Henry V's rant before Harfleur or his injunction to his soldiers to imitate the action of the tiger. It can be because we all have stored up within ourselves so many unrequited wrongs and injuries, forgotten and unforgotten, and beneath these such an inheritance of racial revenge, that we like nothing better than to rid ourselves of a little of the accumulation by projecting it, in a crowd of persons similarly disposed, on the defenseless puppets of the dramatic imagination. There is no mystery about it. Anyone can follow the effect along his own backbone.

But if we are all repositories of racial revenge, we are also repositories of the rarer tendencies that over the centuries have resisted revenge. Against the contagion of a theater audience these ethereal forces have practically no chance, for in the crowd we are bound to take the play as drama rather than as poetry. But in solitude and in silence these forces are sure to lead a certain number of sensitive readers to shudder at the thought of Hamlet shedding blood. Let them express their revulsion, however, and instantly there will be someone to remind them that, whatever may be true now, "in those days" blood revenge was an accepted part of the moral code. As if Shakespeare were a historian and not a poet!

"Those days" never existed. They never existed poetically, I mean. No doubt the code of the vendetta has prevailed in many ages in many lands and revenge has been a favorite theme of the poets from Homer down. History itself, as William James remarked, has been a bath of blood. Yet there is a sense in which the dictum "Thou shalt not kill" has remained just as absolute in the kingdom of the imagination as in the Mosaic law. Moralize bloodshed by custom, legalize it by the state, camouflage it by romance, and still to the finer side of human nature it is just bloodshed; and always where poetry has become purest and risen highest there has been some parting of Hector and Andromache, some lament of the Trojan women, to show that those very deeds of vengeance and martial glory that the poet himself is ostensibly glorifying have somehow failed to utter the last word. To utter that last word—or try to—is poetry's ultimate function, to defend man against his own brutality, against

> That monster, custom, who all sense doth eat,
> Of habits devil,

a much emended line-and-a-half of Hamlet that makes excellent sense exactly as it stands.

If Shakespeare was bent in this play on presenting the morality of a primitive time, why did he make the mistake of centering it around a man who in endowment is as far ahead of either the Elizabethan age or our own as the code of blood revenge is behind both? "The ultimate fact is," says J. M. Robertson, "that Shakespeare *could not* make a psychologically or otherwise consistent play out of a plot which retained a strictly barbaric action while the hero was transformed into a supersubtle Elizabethan." *Hamlet,* the conclusion is, is a failure because the materials Shakespeare inherited were too tough and intractable. Too tough and intractable for what? That they were too tough and intractable for a credible historical picture may be readily granted. But what of it? And since when was poetry supposed to defer to history? Two world wars in three decades ought to have taught us that our history has not gone deep enough. But poetry has. The greatest poetry has always depicted the world as a little citadel of nobility threatened by an immense barbarism, a flickering candle surrounded by infinite night. The "historical" impossibility of *Hamlet* is its poetical truth, and the paradox of its central figure is the universal psychology of man.

Yet, in the face of the correspondingly universal fascination that both the play and its hero have exercised, T. S. Eliot can write: "*Hamlet,* like the sonnets, is full of some stuff that the writer could not drag to light, contemplate, or manipulate into art. We must simply admit that here Shakespeare tackled a problem which proved too much for him. Why he attempted it at all is an insoluble enigma." In which case, why all this fuss over a play that failed? To reason as Eliot does is to indict the taste and intelligence of three centuries. If Hamlet is just a puzzle, why has the world not long since transferred its adulation to Fortinbras and Laertes? They, at any rate, are clear. If action and revenge were what was wanted, they understood them. The trouble is that by no stretch of the imagination can we think of Shakespeare preferring their morality to that of his hero. They are living answers to the contention that Hamlet ought to have done what either of them, in his situation, would have done instantly. For what other purpose indeed did Shakespeare put them in than to make that plain?

But Hamlet himself, it will be said, accepts the code of blood revenge. Why should we question what one we so admire embraces with such unquestioning eagerness? With such *suspicious* eagerness might be closer to the mark. But waiving that for the moment, let us see what is involved in the assumption that Shakespeare thought it was Hamlet's duty to kill the King.

It involves nothing less than the retraction of all the Histories, of *Romeo and Juliet* and *Julius Caesar.* Private injury, domestic feud, civil revolution, imperialistic conquest: one by one in these plays Shakespeare had demonstrated how bloodshed invoked in their name brings on the very thing it was intended to avert, how, like seeds that propagate their own kind, force begets force and vengeance vengeance. And now in *Hamlet* Shakespeare is supposed to say: "I was wrong. I take it all back. Blood should be shed to avenge blood." And more incredible yet, we must picture him a year or two later taking his new opinion back and being reconverted in turn to his original conviction in *Othello, Macbeth, King Lear,* and the rest. If you find a term in a mathematical series fitting perfectly between what has gone before and what follows, you naturally assume it is in its right place, as you do a piece that fits into the surrounding pieces in a jigsaw puzzle. Only on the assumption that Hamlet ought not to have killed the King can the play be fitted into what then becomes the unbroken progression of Shakespeare's spiritual development. The only other way out of the difficulty for those who do not themselves believe in blood revenge is to hold that Shakespeare in *Hamlet* is an archeologist or anthropologist interested in the customs of primitive society rather than a poet concerned with the eternal problems of man.

"But in that case why didn't Shakespeare make his intention clear?" A question that implies a profound misapprehension of the nature of poetic, if not of dramatic, art.

Of course Shakespeare expected his audience to assume that Hamlet should kill the King, exactly as he expected them to assume that Katharine was a shrew, and that Henry V was a glorious hero for attempting to steal the kingdom of France. He was not so ignorant of human nature as not to know how it reacts under the stimulus of primitive emotion. He understood too that what ought to be can be seen only against a background of what is. Carlyle spoke of the Paolo and Francesca incident in *The Inferno* as a thing woven of rainbows on a background of eternal black. And Hamlet himself declared:

> I'll be your foil, Laertes; in mine ignorance
> Your skill shall, like a star i' the darkest night,
> Stick fiery off indeed.

The contrast need not always be so extreme. The setting is more ordinarily terrestrial and diurnal than infernal, or even nocturnal. If, enthralled by its familiarity, we do not alter the focus of our eyes to see what may be unfamiliar and perhaps nearly invisible in the foreground, how is that the poet's fault? That is not his lookout. His business is to create a work of art. How it is taken is not his responsibility. "Here it is," he seems to say, as perhaps God did when he made the world, "take it, and see what you can make of it." And different men make very different things. To all of us in life appearances are deceitful. To all save the wisest characters in a work of dramatic art, if it be true to life, they should be even more so. The spectator or reader of that work takes delight in their delusions. But meanwhile from a higher level the poet may be deluding him. Living would lose all its challenge if everything were made so plain that anybody could understand it all the first time. And so would reading. You plunge into a poem as you plunge into battle — at your peril. "That which can be made explicit to the idiot," said Blake, "is not worth my care."

This procedure is not trickery. Even the alertest reader must be partly taken in the first time or he will miss more then he gains. A book that can be comprehended at a first reading is not imaginative literature. Dostoevsky's novels, for instance, contain many dreams and hallucinations which the reader is intended to mistake for occurrences in the objective world until, later, he realizes that the person having the experience was asleep or in a trance. That is as it should be. For dreams are true while they last, and Dostoevsky's technique leads us to identify ourselves with the dreamer. A too critical reader who sees through the device deprives himself of the very experience he would understand. Intellectuals cannot read. A child lost in a story is the model of right first reading. The more ingenuous we are the first time the better. But not the second and third times. Then the critical intellect should begin to check the imagination — or check on it rather. Shakespeare, I am convinced, wanted us at first to believe that Hamlet ought to kill the King in order that we might undergo his agony with him. But he did not want us, I am equally convinced, to persist in that belief. We must view Hamlet first under the aspect of time so that later we may view him under the aspect of eternity. We must be him before we can understand him.

And here, oddly, we have an advantage over Shakespeare. The author of *Hamlet,* when he wrote it, had not had the privilege of reading *King Lear* and other post-Hamletian masterpieces. But we have had it, and can read *Hamlet* in their light. This does not mean that we import into *Hamlet* from later plays anything that is not already there. A work of art must stand or fall by itself. It merely means that, with vision sharpened by later plays, we are enabled to see in *Hamlet* what was already there but hidden from us — as a later dream does not alter an earlier one but may render it intelligible because of a mutual relation. In some sense or other, as we have seen, Hamlet's problem must have been Shakespeare's. He doubtless wrote the play in part to make that problem clear, just as Tolstoy, to make his problem clear, wrote *Anna Karenina. Hamlet* being only a step in its solution, its author could not conceivably have caught its full import at once. But we can see, as later he could see, whither it was tending, as a prophecy is remembered and illuminated when it is fulfilled. However much above us Shakespeare may be in genius, at any particular moment in his development we are beyond him in time. To that extent we are on the mountain while he is on the road.

And even if we do not look beyond *Hamlet,* our vantage point enables us to see from the past the direction that road was taking. Roads, to be sure, may make unexpected turns, and even a long-maintained general course is no guarantee against its interruption. But highways of Shakespearean breadth seldom go off abruptly at right angles. And so it is permissible to ask as we come to *Hamlet:* What, judging from what he had been doing, might Shakespeare be expected to do next?

The answer is plain. Having given us in Hal-Henry (not to mention Romeo and Richard II) a divided man easily won by circumstances to the side of violence, and in Brutus a man so won only after a brief but terrible inner struggle, what then? Why, naturally, the next step in the progression: a divided man won to the side of violence only after a protracted struggle. And this is precisely what we have in Hamlet. Moreover, there is a passage in the play that confirms just this development. Indeed, as the word "development" suggests, a better metaphor than the road is the figure of an unfolding organism.

In the notes Dostoevsky made when composing *The Brothers Karamazov* there is one especially remarkable revelation: the fact that in its earliest stages the hero, who was to become Alyosha, is identified with the hero of a previous novel, *The Idiot,* being even called the Idiot by name. It shows how akin to the dream the creative faculty is — one character splitting off from another. What was at first a vague differentation ends as a distinct individual, but an individual always bearing traces of his origin, as traces of the parent can be found in the child and in the man.

Shakespeare is not Dostoevsky, and it is not likely that an early draft of *Hamlet* will ever be found in which the Prince's name is first set down as Brutus.

Yet there is a bit of dialogue in the play as we have it that links the two almost as intimately as Alyosha is linked with Prince Myshkin. The passage is brief and apparently parenthetical. Shortly before the performance of *The Murder of Gonzago*, Hamlet suddenly addresses Polonius:

> HAMLET: My lord, you played once i' the university, you say?
> POLONIUS: That did I, my lord, and was accounted a good actor.
> HAMLET: What did you enact?
> POLONIUS: I did enact Julius Caesar: I was killed i' the Capitol;
> Brutus killed me.
> HAMLET: It was a brute part of him to kill so capital a calf there.

It is interesting, to begin with, that Polonius was accounted a good actor in his youth. He has been playing a part ever since, until his mask has become a part of his face. The roles that men cast themselves for often reveal what they are and may prophesy what they will become. That Polonius acted Julius Caesar characterizes both men: Caesar, the synonym of imperialism, Polonius, the petty domestic despot — the very disparity of their kingdoms makes the comparison all the more illuminating.

But it is not just Caesar and Polonius. Brutus is mentioned too. And Brutus killed Caesar. In an hour or so Hamlet is to kill Polonius. If Polonius is Caesar, Hamlet is Brutus. This is the rehearsal of the deed. For to hate or scorn is to kill a little. "It was a brute part . . . to kill so capital a calf there." The unconscious is an inveterate punster and in that "brute part" Hamlet passes judgment in advance on his own deed in his mother's chamber. Prophecy, rehearsal, judgment: was ever more packed into fewer words? *Et tu*, Hamlet?

And it is not Brutus only who stands behind Hamlet. There is another behind him. And another behind *him*.

> A third is like the former. . . .
> A fourth! start, eyes!
> What! will the line stretch out to the crack of doom?
> Another yet!

We need not follow it as far as did Macbeth to perceive that, as Hamlet listens to the spirit of his father, behind him are the ghosts of Brutus, Hal, and Romeo. "Beware, Hamlet," says Romeo, "my soul told me to embrace Juliet and with her all the Capulets. But my 'father' bade me kill Tybalt and carry on the hereditary quarrel. And I obeyed him." "Beware, Hamlet," says Hal, "my soul told me to hold fast to Falstaff's love of life. But, instead, I did what is expected of a king, rejected Falstaff, and following my dying father's advice, made war on France." "Beware, Hamlet," says Brutus, "Portia and my soul gave ample warning. But

Cassius reminded me that there was once a Brutus who expelled a tyrant from Rome, and, in the name of 'our fathers,' tempted me to exceed him in virtue by killing one. And I did. Beware, Hamlet." Each of these men wanted to dedicate himself to life. Romeo wanted to love. Hal wanted to play. Brutus wanted to read philosophy. But in each case a commanding hand was placed on the man's shoulder that disputed the claim of life in the name of death. Romeo defied that command for a few hours, and then circumstances proved too strong for him. Hal evaded it for a while, and then capitulated utterly. Brutus tried to face the issue, with the result of civil war within himself. But death won. Brutus' suppressed compunctions, however, ejected themselves in the form of a ghost that, Delphically, was both Caesar and Brutus' own evil spirit, his reliance on force.

Hamlet is the next step. He is a man as much more spiritually gifted than Brutus as Brutus is than Hal. The story of Hamlet is the story of Hal over again, subtilized, amplified, with a different ending. The men themselves seem so unlike that the similarities of their situations and acts are obscured. Like Hal, Hamlet is a prince of charming quality who cares nothing at the outset for his royal prospects but is absorbed in playing and savoring life. Only with him it is playing in a higher sense: dramatic art, acting, and playwriting rather than roistering in taverns and perpetrating practical jokes. And, like all men genuinely devoted to art, he is deeply interested in philosophy and religion, drawing no sharp lines indeed between or among the three. Because he is himself an imaginative genius, he needs no Falstaff to spur him on. Hamlet is his own Falstaff.

Hamlet's father, like Hal's, was primarily concerned with war, and after death calls his son to a deed of violence, not to imperial conquest, as the elder Henry did, but to revenge. Like Hal, Hamlet accepts the injunction. But instead of initiating a change that gradually alters him into his father's likeness, the decision immediately shakes his being to its foundations. The "antic disposition" under which he hides his real design is an exaggerated counterpart of the "wildness" under which Hal had previously concealed his own political ambition—however much less selfish and better grounded Hamlet's deception was.

The far more shattering effect on Hamlet than on Hal or even on Brutus of the task he assumes shows how much more nearly balanced are the opposing forces in his case. Loyalty to his father and the desire to grow unto himself—thirst for revenge and thirst for creation—are in Hamlet almost in equilibrium, though of course he does not know it. Henry V was vaguely troubled by nocturnal stirrings of the spirit. He saw no ghost. Brutus became the victim of insomnia. He stifled his conscience by action and saw no ghost until after the deed. Hamlet saw his before the deed—as Brutus would have if his soul had been stronger—and it made night hideous for him. No spirit but one from below would have produced that effect, and the fact that "this fellow in the cellarage" speaks from under the platform when he echoes Hamlet's "swear" is in keeping with Shakespeare's frequent use of the symbolism that associates what is physically low with what is morally wrong. Hamlet's delay, then, instead of giving ground for condemnation, does him credit. It shows his soul is still alive and will not submit to the demands of the father without a struggle. If two forces pulling a body in opposite directions are unequal, the body will move in response to the preponderant force. If the two are nearly equal, but alternately gain slight ascendancy, it will remain unmoved except for corresponding vibrations. In a tug of war between evenly matched teams the rope at first is almost motionless, but ultimately the strength of one side ebbs and then the rope moves suddenly and violently. So mysterious, and no more, is Hamlet's hesitation, followed, as it finally was, by lightning-like action. "Shakespeare, as everyone knows," says Dover Wilson, "never furnishes an explanation for Hamlet's inaction." "No one knows," says Professor Alden, "why Hamlet delays." And many others have said the same. Yet Shakespeare puts in the mouth of Claudius words that seem expressly inserted to explain the riddle. The King, caught in the same way between opposing forces—desire to keep the fruits of his sin and desire to pray—declares:

> And, like a man to double business bound,
> I stand in pause where I shall first begin,
> And both neglect.

That seems plain enough. But what is true of Claudius in this one scene is true of Hamlet during all the earlier part of the play. It is as if his soul were a body in space so delicately poised between the gravitation of the earth and the gravitation, or we might say the levitation, of the sun that it "hesitates" whether to drop into the one or fly up to the other. It sometimes seems as if *Homo sapiens* were in just that situation.

People who think Shakespeare was just a playwright say Hamlet delayed that there might be a five-act play! Others, who calmly neglect much of the text, say he delayed because of external obstacles. Coleridge thinks it was because he thought too much. Bradley, because he was so melancholy. It would be nearer the truth to say he thought too much and was melancholy because he delayed. The more powerful an unconscious urge, the stronger and the more numerous the compensations and rationalizations with which consciousness attempts to fight it. Hence the excess of thought and feeling. Goethe, I would say, is far closer to the mark than Coleridge and Bradley in attributing Hamlet's hesitation to a feminine element in the man. But then he proceeds to spoil it all by implying that Hamlet is weak and effeminate: "a lovely, pure and most moral nature, without the strength of nerve that makes a hero, sinks beneath a burden which it cannot bear and must not cast away." The implication is that Hamlet ought to have killed the King at once; also that loveliness, purity, and moral insight are not sources of strength and heroism!

On the contrary, they are the very higher heroism that challenges a more primitive one in this play. Hamlet is the battlefield where the two meet. It is war in that psychological realm where all war begins. Hamlet is like Thermopylae, the battle that stands first among all battles in the human imagination because of its symbolic quality — a contest between the Persian hordes of the lower appetites and the little Greek band of heroic instinct.

They have the numbers, we, the heights.

At Thermopylae the Persians won. Yet we think of it as a Greek victory because it was the promise of Salamis and Plataea. So with Hamlet. Hamlet lost. But *Hamlet* is the promise of *Othello* and *King Lear*. . . .

At last Hamlet has killed the King.
But has he?
When we look back, everything converges to answer that question with those two words of the Prince's own: "Never Hamlet."

Never Hamlet!
If Hamlet from himself be ta'en away.

But who, then, did kill the King, if not Hamlet?
Why! his rashness, his indiscretion, the divinity "of hell" that shaped his end, fortune, fate, "this water," the Devil. Shakespeare has been at pains to supply an abundance of answers, as if to show how important he considered the question.

It is just as it was with Romeo in the two duels in *Romeo and Juliet*. From the viewpoint of drama we have only approval for Hamlet's conduct in this scene, his sending to death the two plotters against his own life. What else could he have done? Was he not acting in self-defense? But at the elevation of poetry, from which we see not just this scene but the action in its entirety, it is another matter. As Romeo descended to the level of Mercutio in killing Tybalt, Hal to the level of his father in invading France, Brutus to the level of Cassius in murdering Caesar, so Hamlet here finally descends to the level of Laertes. With the rapiers, he once for all exchanges fairness for venom. This duel, like so many duels in literature, is symbolic, condensing into a sudden image the meaning of the play. Under a provocation that, this time, seems like necessity, Hamlet repeats the pattern he cut out for himself at the crisis in the play scene: he converts art — in this case the art of fencing — into death. It is now too late to blame him. Hamlet's mistake, like those of the other characters just mentioned, was made far back, while he was still free. From the moment when, trembling with suppressed excitement, he interrupted *The Murder of Gonzago* by crying out:

> He poisons him i' the garden for's estate,

to his final

> Then, venom, to thy work!

an unbroken chain of reflex actions—of which the killing of Polonius and the sending of Rosencrantz and Guildenstern to their doom are the most conspicuous—all tend to one conclusion: that the killing of the King was as purely an instinctive act as is that by which a man draws back his hand from fire.

> The lion dying thrusteth forth his paw.

Hamlet's deed was like that. It was not divinity shaping man's end; it was man, under the compulsion of circumstance, imitating the action of the tiger. And the thrill we get in the theater as the King falls—from which not a single spectator, I believe, is exempt—is not a celestial one. We take the deed *there* as a noble act finally accomplished. It is only afterward, when we recollect it in tranquillity, that we recognize its senseless and fatalistic character. Indeed, in spite of differences, the situation resembles the one where Richard II runs amuck and kills the assistants of Exton. It was desperation, not bravery, that prompted Richard's act. A second later, Exton in turn strikes him down, only to realize the next second what he has done and to wish it undone:

> For now the devil, that told me I did well,
> Says that this deed is chronicled in hell.

It is not at the moment of action, but afterward, that we see. And that can be as true of the theater as of life.

But we left the action at its climax.

Laertes begs Hamlet's forgiveness and follows the King. Hamlet, as if visited by his own genius at the end, speaks to those around him as if they were gathered in a theater as "audience to this act," prevents Horatio from drinking the last drops of the poisoned liquor, and cries to his friend in words the whole world knows by heart:

> Absent thee from felicity awhile,
> And in this harsh world draw thy breath in pain,
> To tell my story.

Martial music is heard in the distance, and a salute. The conquering Fortinbras has come from Poland, and Hamlet has just enough breath left to give him his dying voice as his successor. What irony! Like Henry V's, all the Elder Hamlet's conquests have been for nothing—for less than nothing. Fortinbras, his former enemy, is to inherit the kingdom! Such is the end to which the Ghost's thirst for vengeance has led.

For Hamlet "the rest is silence." The tragedy is summed up in the contrast between those four mysterious words and Horatio's

> Good-night, sweet prince,
> And flights of angels sing thee to thy rest!

Fortinbras, who has now entered, gazes around him as on a battlefield:

> This quarry cries on havoc. O proud death!
> What feast is toward in thine eternal cell,
> That thou so many princes at a shot
> So bloodily hast struck?

And Horatio promises to tell, in explanation,

> Of carnal, bloody, and unnatural acts,
> Of accidental judgements, casual slaughters,
> Of deaths put on by cunning and forc'd cause,
> And, in this upshot, purposes mistook
> Fall'n on the inventors' heads.

The Ghost's words sounded eloquent and noble when he was clamoring for revenge. This is their harvest.

The dead Hamlet is borne out "like a soldier" and the last rites over his body are to be the rites of war. The final word of the text is "shoot." The last sounds we hear are a dead march and the reverberations of ordnance being shot off. The end crowns the whole. The sarcasm of fate could go no further. Hamlet, who aspired to nobler things, is treated at death as if he were the mere image of his father: a warrior. Shakespeare knew what he was about in making the conclusion of his play martial. Its theme has been war as well as revenge. It is the story of the Minotaur over again, of that monster who from the beginning of human strife has exacted his annual tribute of youth. No sacrifice ever offered to it was more precious than Hamlet. But he was not the last.

If ever a play seems expressly written for the twentieth century, it is *Hamlet*. It should be unnecessary to underscore its pertinence to an age in which, twice within three decades, the older generation has called on the younger generation to settle a quarrel with the making of which it had nothing to do. So taken, *Hamlet* is an allegory of our time. Imagination or violence, Shakespeare seems to say, there is no other alternative. They are the two forces that exact obedience, the one freely, the other under compulsion. Art or war: it is the only choice humanity ever had or ever will have. Unless the first is resorted to while we are free, the other has to be resorted to under the pressure of events. Hamlet made the right choice, but then, at the moment of triumph, converted an instrument of regeneration into an instrument of revenge. Made for heaven, he was tempted by hell—and fell.

The prime requisite for an understanding of *Hamlet* is a belief in ghosts. The common reader who has that will come nearer its heart than the most learned man who lacks it—just as a youth of seventeen who is in love is better fitted to comprehend the *Divine Comedy* than a scholar who has spent a lifetime on it but who has never shared the experience on which it is based. If "a belief in ghosts" sounds too old-fashioned or superstitious, call it, more pedantically, a belief in the autonomous character of the unconscious. The two are the same.

Dover Wilson has written of the belief in spirits of Catholics and Protestants in Shakespeare's day. Catholics, he tells us, held that ghosts came from Purgatory and were actually souls of the departed. Protestants thought they came from hell (or rarely from heaven) and were devils (or angels) who had assumed the shape and appearance of the dead.

I once asked a young girl (barely over the border of childhood) to whom I had read *Hamlet*, whether she thought the Ghost was Hamlet's father or the devil. I like to get the fresh reaction of innocence to a masterpiece, uncontaminated by traditional critical opinion. "I don't see that it makes any difference," she said, "I should think it would be just the same." "Just the same?" I inquired, arrested. "Well," she explained, "I should think that whoever told you to kill somebody was the devil." *Just the same:* in a flash those three words show that the Catholic and Protestant views that Wilson discriminates are really one. The Father, in so far as he represents authority and force, *is* the Devil, a power utterly transcending anything human in any common meaning of that term. Shakespeare here, as usual, is a harmonizer of opposites.

But it is not just Shakespeare and childhood who agree. The poets have always seen that the supreme question for humanity is the existence of the gods— and devils. Their existence and their incidence in human affairs. It is startling to compare one or two of their utterances with Shakespeare's.

Go back to Aeschylus, the first of the supreme Greek dramatists. Clytemnestra is speaking of her slaying of her husband, Agamemnon:

> And criest thou still this deed hath been
> My work? Nay, gaze, and have no thought

> That this is Agamemnon's Queen.
> 'Tis He, 'tis He, hath round him wrought
> This phantom of the dead man's wife;
> He, the Old Wrath, the Driver of Men Astray,
> Pursuer of Atreus for the feast defiled;
> To assoil an ancient debt he hath paid this life;
> A warrior and a crowned King this day
> Atones for a slain child.

Or come down, past Shakespeare, almost to our own day, to Dostoevsky. Raskolnikov is speaking of the murder of the Old Pawnbroker:

> Did I murder the old woman? I murdered myself, not her! I crushed myself once for all, for ever. . . . But it was the devil that killed that old woman, not I.

And then go back to Shakespeare, to Hamlet. He is apologizing for the slaying of Polonius:

> Was't Hamlet wronged Laertes? Never Hamlet!
> If Hamlet from himself be ta'en away,
> And when he's not himself does wrong Laertes,
> Then Hamlet does it not, Hamlet denies it.
> Who does it then? His madness. If't be so,
> Hamlet is of the faction that is wrong'd;
> His madness is poor Hamlet's enemy.

Or to the First Gravedigger:

> But if the water come to him, and drown him, he drowns not himself.

The Old Wrath, the Devil, Madness, the Water, Whoever Tells You To Kill: what difference does the terminology make? Each of these words or phrases is just another name for the infernal forces which, unless warded off by an eternal vigilance, rush in at the slightest abdication of his own freedom, to possess man. (To the celestial forces that can take possession of him Shakespeare was to turn his attention more and more in the plays that follow *Hamlet.*) Perhaps the profoundest and certainly the most detailed analysis of this idea in modern literature is *The Possessed* of Dostoevsky, or *The Devils,* as the title of the novel should properly be translated. But probably Orestes from ancient literature, and Ivan Karamazov from recent, are the two most interesting single figures to place beside Hamlet. Orestes murdered his mother, went mad, and was pursued by the Furies. Hamlet was visited by his Father, played with murderous thoughts, and committed irresponsible acts. Ivan Karamazov played with murderous thoughts, was visited by the Devil, and went insane. "God will conquer!" cried Alyosha Karamazov in the critical hour when his brother's mind hung in the balance, "he will rise up in the light of truth, or . . . he'll perish in hate, revenging on himself and on everyone his having served the cause he does not believe in." So with Hamlet. He is that second alternative. God did not conquer, and Hamlet wreaked revenge on himself and on everyone for having served the cause he did not believe in, the cause of blood revenge.

In *War and Peace,* Tolstoy gives us the same situation with the other outcome. Pierre, like Brutus, conceives it to be his duty to kill a tyrant: Napoleon. Like Hamlet, he wanders about in a daze. "He was suffering the anguish men suffer," says Tolstoy, "when they persist in undertaking a task impossible for them — not from its inherent difficulties, but from its incompatibility with their own nature." But at the critical moment there is a child in a burning building. Pierre dashes in to save her and in doing so saves himself. He is purged from his mad resolve. Nor is it just the heroism of the act that does it. It is its symbolism no less. In saving the actual child from the literal fire, he saves his own innocence, the child within himself, from the criminal fire that threatens to consume him. Imagination triumphs over force.

It is interesting to speculate on what might have occurred if some happy chance or good angel had intervened in Hamlet's case as it did in Pierre's. Suppose for a moment that Hamlet had let *The Murder of Gonzago* take its unhindered way, and imagine further that the miracle happened: that Claudius repented and surrendered the throne to Hamlet. What might have followed?

Such conjectures are idle enough, and I should not be recording any of mine here if by chance I had not discovered that one of Shakespeare's own contemporaries, a man who had seen and perhaps known him in the flesh, had cherished an idea curiously similar to one of my own, not precisely about Hamlet, to be sure, but about what I may call the Hamletian Shakespeare.

Suppose Hamlet had taken over the throne of Denmark. The Prince as King: is it hard to conceive him in that role? Fortinbras at any rate did not think so:

> For he was likely, had he been put on,
> To have prov'd most royally.

One thing certainly we can count on: he would have made a most unconventional monarch. He would have been just about everything the rest of Shakespeare's kings were not.

In the first place, he had what ought to be the prime negative requisite for those in high position the world over, what only Henry VI of Shakespeare's kings in the History Plays possessed: no love of power. It is precisely because those who are greedy for power so often get it that power is so often administered in the interest of greed. Except for a couple of passages near the end of the play that are mere rationalizations of his hatred of his uncle, there is nothing to indicate that Claudius' usurpation of the throne, as such, ever caused Hamlet so much as one wakeful night. He was interested in higher things than governing—and for that very reason was fitted to govern. Again, with the same exception of Henry VI, all Shakespeare's kings welcomed, by daylight at least, the ceremonies of royalty. They enjoyed being lifted by "degree" above their natural station. Hamlet disdained all such trappings and went to the other extreme of debasing himself from Prince to madman. He practiced to the point of perversion by daylight what Henry V only soliloquized about by night.

Secondly: Hamlet had the love and confidence of the people. Twice Claudius refers to this:

> Yet must we not put the strong law on him:
> He's loved of the distracted multitude,

and

> The other motive,
> Why to a public count I might not go,
> Is the great love the general gender bear him,
> Who, dipping all his faults in their affection,
> Would, like the spring that turneth wood to stone,
> Convert his gyves to graces.

The History Plays discriminated the commons as a group of individuals, from the mob as a pack of wolves. So here. The love of the people for Hamlet is thrown in contrast with the backing by the rabble of Laertes, a love that aroused the same jealousy in Claudius as a similar affection for Rosalind—that feminine Hamlet over whom the cloud never fell—did in the Duke in *As You Like It*.

Thirdly: Hamlet had the creative instinct and capacity to alter the royal occupation from what it always has been, war, to what it ought to be, art: not "art" as amusement or distraction, but art in its deepest and most religious sense. "Empire against art," said Blake, putting it in three words. If a Falstaffian Hal could have taught England to play in the common acceptation of the term, Hamlet could have taught Denmark to play in a deeper creative sense.

What Hamlet's succession might have meant may be seen by asking: What if, on the death of Elizabeth, not James of Scotland but William of Stratford had inherited the throne! That would have been England falling before William the Conqueror indeed. And it did so fall in the sense that, ever since, Shakespeare has been England's imaginative king, who has taught more men and women to play perhaps than any other man in the history of the world. But if the England of his own day could have crowned him more specifically, by following his spirit, it might have found its way between the Scylla of a decadent Renaissance and the Charybdis of a puritanical reformation and revolution. It might have substituted freedom and imagination for luxury and dogma. And so might Denmark have achieved a similar consummation under Hamlet, even if he had worn no crown, instead of condemning itself, as all the kingdoms of the world have condemned themselves in the past, to a perpetual oscillation between the softness of a Claudius and the hardness of a Fortinbras.

Browsing one day among Elizabethan allusions to Shakespeare, I ran on these lines of John Davies of Hereford:

> *To our English Terence, Mr. Will Shake-speare*
> Some say (good Will) which I, in sport, do sing
> Had'st thou not plaid some kingly parts in sport,
> Thou hadst been a companion for a *king:*
> And beene a king among the meaner sort.
> Some others raile; but, raile as they think fit,
> Thou hast no rayling, but a reigning wit:
>> And honesty thou sow'st, which they do reape:
>> So to increase their stocke which they do keepe:

Shakespeare — so John Davies of Hereford believed — was fit to be a king of the common people. He still is. He is an unfallen Hamlet.

An Explication
of the Player's Speech

Harry Levin

The text before us is a purple passage, not because it has been admired, but because it stands out from the rest of the play. On the whole it has aroused, in Shakespearean commentators, less admiration than curiosity and less curiosity than bewilderment. Some of them, like Polonius, have been quite frankly bored with it; many of them, unlike Hamlet himself, have considered it highly bombastic. Those who discern the hand of another playwright, whenever Shakespeare's writing presents a problem, have fathered it upon Marlowe, Chapman, Kyd, and even unlikelier authors. Others, hesitating to assume that Shakespeare would cite a fellow playwright at such length, have interpreted the speech as parody or satire—although who is being parodied, or what is being satirized, or how or why, is again a matter of diverging opinion. Still others have explained the incongruity, between these high-pitched lines and the ordinary dialogue, by assuming that Shakespeare had taken occasion to foist upon his patient audience a fragment of his earlier journeywork. As Guildenstern says of that theatrical controversy which accounted for the presence of the Players at Elsinore: "O, there has been much throwing about of brains." More rigorous scholarship tends to support the integrity of Shakespeare's text, just as more perceptive criticism emphasizes the consciousness of his artistry. Appealing to the authority of Sir Edmund Chambers, as well as to the insight of A. C. Bradley, we can proceed from the assumption that the passage at hand is both authentic and advised. But is it well advised? is it really significant? and what, if so, does it signify?

We can scarcely become aware of its significance without some preliminary

From *The Question of Hamlet.* © 1959 by Oxford University Press.

awareness of its context: not only the intrinsic place that it occupies within the dramatic economy of *Hamlet,* but the stream of extrinsic associations that it carries along with it into the drama. The player who, at Hamlet's request, gives us this demonstration of his professional skill, this "taste" of his "quality," is cast in a functional role; for in the next act he and his fellows are destined to perform the play that will "catch the conscience of the King." Meanwhile Shakespeare, who seldom misses an opportunity to talk about his craft, indulges in two of his fullest discussions on the theater. These are often regarded as digressions, and one of them is usually cut on the stage. There is indeed a ludicrous German adaptation which, omitting the Player's speech altogether, transfers the name of its protagonist, Pyrrhus, to the character of the King (*alias* Gonzago) in the play-within-the-play. But Goethe, who took a producer's point of view, saw how that "passionate speech" served a psychological purpose by planting the suggestion in Hamlet's mind that leads to his experiment upon Claudius. And the late Harley Granville-Barker, perhaps the most pragmatic of all Shakespeareans, observed that the name of Hecuba was not only a necessary link between the First Player's scene and Hamlet's ensuing soliloquy, but also an implicit commentary on the Queen. To underline that observation: if the Player is nothing to Hecuba, or she to him, it follows *a fortiori* that Hamlet should feel and show a much deeper grief, and that Gertrude has failed abysmally to live up to the standard of royal motherhood.

What attracted Hamlet to this particular selection, from a play which he presumably had witnessed at its single performance, is as easy to understand as why he mentions Jephta to Polonius. It is harder for modern readers to square his description of it with the specimen from it that follows; though the lines are said to contain no "sallets" and the matter no affectation, the style is heavily conceited and the subject undeniably sensational. Yet Hamlet's famous excuse for the play's indifferent reception ("'twas caviary to the general") runs curiously parallel to the publisher's complaint that *Troilus and Cressida* was "never clapper-clawed by the palms of the vulgar." The latter play is intimately linked to the fragment from *Hamlet* by their common theme, as well as by the turgid phrases and nervous rhythms that run through both. Coleridge, following A. W. Schlegel as usual, and followed by Bradley as usual, described the phraseology that Hamlet applauded as "the language of lyric vehemence and epic pomp, and not of the drama." Dryden, whose attitude toward poetic diction was rather more prosaic, distinguished between "true sublimity" and what, in this instance, he labeled "the blown puffy style." He tried to deal gently with Shakespeare by denying him the authorship of the tirade, which he quoted as "an example of expressing passion figuratively." And, being rather more than a closet dramatist, he realized that the lines in question were not undramatic but melodramatic:

> to say nothing without a metaphor, a simile, an image, or description, is, I doubt, to smell a little too strongly of the buskin.

However contrived, such contrivance lends an epic sweep to Shakespeare's more restricted medium. By requesting the account of "Priam's slaughter" as it was told in "Aeneas' tale to Dido," Hamlet refers us to what might be called the official version: the retrospective story that Vergil tells in the second book of his *Aeneid* (506–58). This material, which the Earl of Surrey had utilized when he first experimented with English blank verse, was rendered more or less straightforwardly by Marlowe and Nashe in their early tragedy, *Dido, Queen of Carthage*. But *Dido* does not seem to have influenced *Hamlet*: the single possible echo that editors note is based on a problematic emendation of Marlowe's text (II.i.254). Further and closer scrutiny of Shakespeare's treatment reveals that — although he elaborated a few small Vergilian details, such as the useless sword ("inutile ferrum") — he is actually less indebted to Vergil than to his favorite among the Latin poets, Ovid. When Lucentio pretends to be a schoolmaster in *The Taming of the Shrew* (III.i.-27–37), he offers Bianca an unblushingly free translation of a couplet describing Troy from Ovid's *Heroides* (I.33–34). When literary narration supplements the bloody action of *Titus Andronicus*, Aeneas' tale to Dido is twice evoked (III.ii.27–28; v.iii.80–87); but then, when the schoolboy alludes to the madness of Hecuba, the book he happens to drop is Ovid's *Metamorphoses* (IV.i. 20–21). Now it so happens that this very poem includes an unforgettable account of her metamorphosis (xiii.488–575), and that the relevant extract figured in Elizabethan schoolbooks as a stock example of "copiousness" — that is to say, variety of expression in conveying emotion.

In shifting his attention from Priam to Hecuba, and his source from Vergil to Ovid, Shakespeare turns from the sphere of the epic to the lyric, and from events to emotions. It is Ovid, too, who inspires his final appeal to the gods themselves: *"illius fortuna deos quoque moverat omnes"* ["her sad fortune moved all the gods"]. But the lyrical note can prevail no more than the epical, since Shakespeare's form is basically tragic; and here his classical model is indicated when Polonius, introducing the Players, warns: "Seneca cannot be too heavy." From "English Seneca read by candlelight," according to Thomas Nashe, playwrights were lifting handfuls — or were they *Hamlets?* — of "tragical speeches." These were couched in what Bottom the Weaver calls "Ercles' vein, a tyrant's vein," the vein touched upon by Shakespeare's Player when he conjures with fortune, darkness, blood, and hell. The tone of his speech is that of the *nuntius*, the Senecan messenger who enters to make a morbidly protracted recital of bad news from offstage — or, for that matter, the Sergeant in *Macbeth* (I.ii.8–42), whose sanguinary report makes the merciless Macdonwald a blood brother to the rugged Pyrrhus. Among the disheveled heroines of Seneca's tragedies, Hecuba looms particularly large as the archetype of maternal woe and queenly suffering. How she was metamorphosed into a dog, after the destruction of Troy, is recollected when, in Seneca's *Agamemnon*, she "barketh as a bedlem bitch about her strangled chylde." The *Troades*, in which she enacts the leading role, is one sustained lamentation, from the death of Priam to the sacrifice of their youngest daughter, the last of Pyrrhus' victims. The Elizabethan translator, pointing the moral, interpolates a chorus of his own:

> If prowes might eternity procure,
> Then Priam yet should live in lyking lust,
> Ay portly pompe of pryde thou art unsure,
> Lo learne by him, O Kinges yee are but dust.
> And Hecuba that wayleth now in care,
> That was so late of high estate a Queene,
> A mirrour is to teach you what you are
> Your wavering wealth, O princes here is seene.

Since the Elizabethans conceived of tragedy as a spectacular descent from the heights to the depths, they could conceive of no more tragic worthies than the King and Queen of Troy. Hence the object-lesson of the first English tragedy, *Gorboduc*, is driven home by identifying the heroine with

> *Hecuba*, the wofullest wretch
> That euer lyued to make a myrrour of.

And in the most popular of all Elizabethan plays, *The Spanish Tragedy*, the hero, instructing a painter to "shew a passion," volunteers to pose for his portrait "like old *Priam* of *Troy*, crying: 'the house is a fire.' But tragedy was more than a sad story of the death of kings and the weeping of tristful queens; it chronicled the fall of dynasties, the destruction of cities, the decline of civilizations. One of the set-pieces in Richard Rainolde's manual, *The Foundacion of Rhetorike* (1563), is entitled "What lamentable Oracion Hecuba Queene of Troie might make, Troie being destroied." European culture, looking backward, looking eastward, looking beyond Greece itself, saw its themes embedded in the primary myth of the Trojan War, and deduced its origins from the historic dispersion that underlay the mythological tradition. Hence even *Hamlet*, which is so deeply rooted in northern saga, has its classical moments: its cross-references to Caesar, Nero, Alexander, to Hercules, Hyperion, Niobe, above all to Pyrrhus, Priam, and Hecuba. Something was rotten in the state of Troy. Hamlet's fellow student at Wittenberg, Marlowe's *Doctor Faustus*, went characteristically farther: into that Gothic atmosphere he projected in the Mediterranean vision of Helen of Troy. Shakespeare caricatured it in *All's Well That Ends Well* (I.iii.74–75), rang changes on it in *Richard II* (IV.i.281–86), and exorcized it in *Troilus and Cressida* (II.ii.81–83). To convert the myth into explicit drama was to break its spell, as Thomas Heywood proved in *The Iron Age* by dramatizing the carnage that Shakespeare narrates and thereby reducing it to absurdity.

The matter of Troy—which Caxton had popularized, which English ballads celebrated, which poets and artists could draw upon as freely as the matter of England itself—served Shakespeare most effectively by helping to frame his characters and outline his situations. It figured upon a tapestry, as it were, backing the literal episodes of English history with a deeper dimension. The conflict between the houses of York and Lancaster was inevitably viewed in the light of the struggle between the Greeks and the Trojans. The father who accidentally slays his son in *3 Henry VI* (II.V.120), like Northumberland when he learns of Hotspur's death in *2 Henry IV* (I.i.70–74), is bound to see himself in Priam's role. Similarly, the Roman mother in *Coriolanus* (I.iii.43–46) and the cursing wife in *Cymbeline* (IV.ii.311–12) associate their grief with Hecuba's. It is not surprising, then, that the impassioned father wants to be painted as Priam in *The Spanish Tragedy*, or that the outraged wife in *The Rape of Lucrece* seeks consolation in a painting of the siege of Troy, more especially in its depiction of Hecuba (1450–51):

> In her the painter had anatomiz'd
> Time's ruin, beauty's wrack, and grim care's reign

When Lucrece surveys the picture, discovering in it a precedent for her sorrows, its dumbness stimulates her to become vocal and its flatness puts her feelings into iconographic relief (1492): "Here feelingly she weeps Troy's painted woes." In similar fashion, all occasions inform against Hamlet, who rediscovers his own plight in the verbal painting, the theatrical mirror of the Player's speech. The narrator, pious Aeneas, recalls him to his filial duty. The King, his father, like Priam, has been slaughtered. The Queen his mother, ironically unlike Hecuba, refuses to play the part of the mourning wife. As for the interloping newcomer—whether you call him Pyrrhus, Neoptolemus, or Fortinbras—he too is prompted by the unquiet ghost of his father, Achilles. His destiny, too, is to bring down the revenge of a dead hero upon the unheroic heads of the living.

II

But these apparitions hover in the background until the words are pronounced that summon them. In moving to the foreground, turning from the context back to the text, our first impression may accord with André Gide's comment: "the meaning of the words is much less significant than the tone and manner of the lines." This is a convenient assumption for one who faces the problems of translating *Hamlet* into French. Happily, since we are not faced with any choice between meaning and manner, we have only to observe what each contributes to the other. Our first observation, once the speech has been detached from the dialogue, is that metrically it seems somewhat more formal than the body of the play. The usual gauge of metrical informality is the proportion of lines that run over or terminate with an extra syllable: the quotient of *Hamlet* as a whole, both for enjambments and for feminine endings, is roughly twenty-three per cent. The run-on lines in this passage (nineteen per cent) are somewhat fewer than the norm, while the off-beat endings (twelve per cent) are hardly more than half the normal percentage. Since the development of the Shakespearean line tends toward an ever-increasing flexibility, the present piece might be relegated to an earlier period on prosodic grounds; but there are other reasons for supposing that Shakespeare here deliberately reverted to a more stilted meter, along with a more artificial tone. Though the cesural pauses are not irregular, the grammar marks them more strongly than the prosody. Out of thirteen sentences, five begin, and one ends, with the line; eight begin, and twelve end, in the middle of a line.

The pulsating effect of these cadences, turbulently beating against conventional restraints, is matched by the diction. A barrage of striking tropes and strained expressions overwhelms the reader or hearer immediately. But a second reading lays bare a basically simple vocabulary, a preponderance of familiar Saxon monosyllables over archaisms, neologisms, technical terms, and Latinate polysyllabics. Three of the lines are entirely monosyllabic (18, 41, 42), with what propriety we can best judge later. The strange words, however, are so farfetched and so strategically placed that they diffuse their strangeness throughout. Ten of them do not occur elsewhere in Shakespeare: "coagulate," "fellies," "hush" (as an adjective), "impasted," "mobled," "o'ersized," "o'erteemed," "repugnant," "unnerved," and "whiff." One of these, "unnerved," seems to be one of Shakespeare's many gifts to the English language. Several others, according to the New English Dictionary, were coined by this speech but never achieved much currency: "impasted," "mobled," "o'ersized," "o'erteemed," and the adjectival "hush." Such idiosyncratic language might provide an argument in favor of non-Shakespearean authorship, were it not counterbalanced at every point — as Bradley has shown — by thoroughly Shakespearean turns of phrase and thought. Even the false start that Hamlet makes at the outset has its significance: "The rugged Pyrrhus, like th'Hyrcanian beast." How that beast, the tiger, goes ramping through Elizabethan drama, as the proverbial embodiment of hardness of heart, a glance at any concordance will show. It cut a meaningful figure in the parting reproaches that Vergil's Dido brought against Aeneas; and, curiously enough, it supplied Robert Greene with an epithet to fling against Shakespeare himself.

After this understandable lapse, Hamlet starts out correctly, and now the cruelty of Pyrrhus is symbolized by his heraldic trappings. Knightly prowess ordinarily finds its outward symbol in armorial panoply, which is frequently contrasted with the reality of blood, sweat, and tears — notably in the characterization of Hotspur. Here, where that situation is reversed, bloodshed is treated as if it were decoration. The sable arms of Pyrrhus resemble his funereal purpose, and also the night—which is not a generic night, but the particular, portentous, claustral night that he and his companions have just spent in the wooden horse. The repeated adjective "black" (2, 4) is an elementary manifestation of evil, like the "Thoughts black" of the poisoner in the play-within-the-play; yet it hints at that "power of blackness" which Melville discerned more fully in Shakespeare's works than anywhere else. But the scene does not appear in its true color until its dark surfaces are "o'ersized" (11), covered with sizing, dripping with redness. Red, unrelieved by quartering, is "total gules" in the unfeeling jargon of heraldry, which Shakespeare deliberately invokes to describe the clotted gore of others shed by Pyrrhus—of parents and children whose family relationships are feelingly specified by way of contrast (7), a contrast which ultimately juxtaposes esthetic and ethical values. He is tricked out, dressed up in the unnatural colors of Marlowe's Tamburlaine—in black and red and in a carbuncular brightness which flickers against the darkness, as opposed to the hues of nature, the blues and browns and greens that Shakespeare has more constantly in mind. Thence the metaphor shifts from light to heat, from visual to tactile images, and to a zeugma which holds in suspension both physical fire and psychological wrath (10). The impasted product of such infernal cookery bears a sinister resemblance to that Senecan pastry in which Titus Andronicus baked his victims.

At this point, the appropriate point where Pyrrhus encounters Priam, the Player takes up the story and—in a manner of speaking—the monologue becomes a dialogue. It should not be forgotten that "anon" (13) is one of those adverbs whose force has been weakened by time: in this case it means "very soon" rather than "later on." It reinforces the series of "nows," which in their turn reinforce the employment of the present tense, and convey the impression of breathless immediacy: we might almost be listening to the play-by-play account of a sporting event. The ineffectuality of the old grandsire's antique sword (15), whose fall prefigures his (19), is motivated by the spirit of general mutiny. The angry swing of his assailant—which, though it goes wild, deprives the father of his remaining strength, unnerves him—rends the air with ten onomatopoetic monosyllables: "But with the whiff and wind of his fell sword" (18). The doublet, "whiff and wind," like the apposition of "bak'd and impasted," is a twist of phrasing which recurs throughout the play: e.g., "Th' expectancy and rose of the fair state." And though the poet hesitates to indulge in a pathetic fallacy, to attribute sensation or sensibility to the city itself, he interprets the crash of its topless towers as a comment on the downfall of its king. Troy, however, has its momentary and metaphorical revenge upon Pyrrhus when the noise, by capturing his ears, arrests his motion. At that fatal moment everything stops; the narrative is transposed to the past tense; and the interjection "lo!" (22) points a moral and pictorial contrast between the bloody tyrant and his "milky" victim (23). Where Lucrece animated a picture with her grief, this episode makes pain endurable by reducing it to two dimensions and setting it in an ornamental frame. The art of painting, almost as frequently as the art of drama, is Hamlet's analogy for the hypocrisies of the court, the discrepancies between appearance and reality.

It is only during this uncharacteristic standstill that Pyrrhus, the unthinking avenger, shows any likeness to his polar opposite, Hamlet. Standing there for the nonce in a cataleptic state of neutrality, as if he had no control over mind or body, equally detached from his intention and his object, he "did nothing"—and the pause is rounded out by an unfilled line (27). Then as he swings into action by way of an epic simile, sight is commingled with sound—or rather, with the absence of sound, since we are asked to visualize a silence (29). And as our gaze is deflected from the clouds to the earth, a second simile takes its departure from the first, and perceives an omen of death in the silent atmosphere (31). Anon— that is, suddenly—like the awaited thunderclap, vengeance is resumed; the retarded decline of the sword (37), with its Homeric reverberation (34), now parallels the dying fall of Priam and of his sword. The word "fall," coming twice in pairs, accentuates the rhythm and underlines the theme. The classical allusion, a preliminary glimpse of "Vulcan's stithy," though somewhat archaically expressed, would be commonplace if it were not for the violence of Shakespeare's application. He uses a favorite stylistic device of his predecessors, the University Wits, who seldom made a comparison without making it invidious: their characters are more beautiful than Venus, as powerful as Jove, no weaker than Hercules. After all, there could be no more remorseless task than to beat out indestructible armor for the god of war. To display as little or less remorse, while striking down a disarmed graybeard, was to be as devoid of sympathy—as ready to inflict suffering and unready to feel it—as any human being could expressibly be.

Dwelling on gross details and imperfections of the flesh ("Eyes without feeling, feeling without sight"), Hamlet will admonish his mother that sense-perception is dulled by sensual indulgence. Here insensibility is communicated by a rhetorical assault upon the senses: primarily "the very faculties of eyes and ears," but incidentally touch and even taste. Leaving the senseless Priam to the insensate Pyrrhus, after another hiatus of half a line (37), the speech addresses violent objurgations to the bitch-goddess Fortune, about whom Hamlet has lately cracked ribald jokes with Rosencrantz and Guildenstern; whose buffets and rewards he prizes Horatio for suffering with equanimity; against whom he will, in the most famous of all soliloquies, be tempted to take arms. An appeal is addressed to the gods, who are envisaged as meeting in epic conclave, to destroy the source of her capricious authority. It is urged that her proverbial wheel, whose revolution determines the ups and downs of individual lives, be itself dismantled; and that its components suffer the destiny to which they have so often carried mortals—to fall, as the angels did in the world's original tragedy, from paradise to hell. To catch the gathering momentum of that descent, Shakespeare again resorts to words of one syllable (not excepting "heav'n"), and relies — as he does throughout — upon assonances and alliterations (41, 42): "And bowl the round nave down the hill of heaven / As far as to the fiends." The same image, that of "a massy wheel," disintegrating as it rolls downhill, is later likened by Rosencrantz to "the cesse of majesty," the death of the king involving "the lives of many" attached to its spokes:

> when it falls,
> Each small annexment, petty consequence,
> Attends the boist'rous ruin.

The fact that the twenty-three foregoing lines (19–42) are frequently omitted from acting versions, notably from the First Quarto, supports the view that they constitute a rhapsodic excursion from the narrative. Shakespeare cleverly obviated boredom on the part of his audience by allowing Polonius to complain and Hamlet to gibe at him. By laughing with Hamlet at Polonius, whose own tediousness is the butt of so many gibes, the audience is pledged to renew its attention. Hamlet, of course, has personal motives for echoing the Player's mention of Hecuba. Thereupon Polonius, who fancies himself as a critic, and who has said of Hamlet's letter to Ophelia that "beautified is a vile phrase," seeks to propitiate Hamlet by voicing judicious approval of a peculiarly inept expression: "Mobled queen is good." Has impressionistic criticism ever said more?

The barefoot queen remains mobled, or muffled, for better or for worse, in spite of editors who prefer "mob-led" or "ennobled." Her special poignance depends upon her abdication of queenly dignity, upon the antitheses between "diadem" (46) and "clout" (45) and between "robe" (46) and "blanket" (48). Shakespeare utilized "blanket" for the very reason that Dr. Johnson sought to exclude it from *Macbeth*: because it degraded what it enveloped, its connotations were neo-classically low. It is also a prefiguration of the "incestuous sheets," the rumpled images of Gertrude's bed, which are constantly lurking in the morbid recesses of Hamlet's imagination. The concept of royalty has been debased: "Hyperion to a satyr," goddess to fishwife. The sword, on its fourth and last appearance, is not unlike a kitchen-knife; while the final outburst of Hecuba is like Homer's portrayal of Helen, in one respect if in no other, since it registers its emotional impact on the spectators. Fortune, it would appear, is still so securely entrenched that the impulse to denounce her is a poisonous subversion of things as they are (50). To appeal once more to the gods is to admit — more skeptically than Ovid — that they may exhibit an Olympian disregard for the whole situation: such is the question that Shakespeare explored in *King Lear*, and which such modern writers as Thomas Hardy have reconsidered. Yet if heaven takes any interest whatsoever in man's affairs, it might be expected to respond to so harassed an incarnation of feminine frailty, and its presumptive response inspires a last downward sweep of sinking metaphor. Its tears, burning like the lurid eyes of Pyrrhus, turning into milk like the revered hair of Priam, and associated by that maternal essence with Hecuba's "o'erteemed loins" (47), might produce a downpour more blinding than her "bisson rheum" (45) and thereby extinguish the holocaust of Troy. What commenced in firelight concludes in rainfall. Recoiling before this bathetic *Götterdämmerung,* Dryden remarks: "Such a sight were indeed enough to have rais'd passion in the Gods, but to excuse the effects of it [the poet] tells you perhaps they did not see it."

III

To break off the speech is to awaken Hamlet from what he calls "a dream of passion" — a glaring nightmare of smoke and screams and ruins — to the light of day. But somber northern daylight renews "the motive and the cue for passion" in his own life, and the Trojan retrospect becomes a Danish omen, joining the echoes of Caesar's assassination and other portents of Hamlet's tragedy. None of the others, however, could have seemed as epoch-making or epoch-shattering as the evocation of Priam, no less a byword for catastrophe to the Elizabethans than the name of Hiroshima seems to us. "O what a fall was there, my countrymen." The catastrophic mood that overtook sensitive Englishmen during the latter years of Elizabeth's reign, particularly after the downfall of Essex, had set the key for the play. From the long-echoing lament of Hecuba, as enunciated by Ovid, Shakespeare had learned the rhetorical lesson of copiousness. It is also probable that his books of rhetoric had taught him an old argument of Quintilian's: that the orator who pens his own speeches would move his hearers more profoundly than the mere elocutionist who recites what someone else has felt and thought and written. At all events, the surface of the drama is undisturbed by the Player's elocution. Again he is merely a player; Polonius is quite unaffected; and Hamlet completes his arrangements for the morrow's performance of the play that will affect Claudius as — it soon appears — this foretaste has affected him. Hitherto constrained from weeping or speaking his mind, he now reveals that the player has wept and spoken for him. The deeply revealing soliloquy that completes the Second Act and sets the scene for the Third, "O what a rogue and peasant slave am I," pulls aside the curtain of heavily figured declamation that has just been spread before us for that very purpose.

To be more precise, the soliloquy is the mirror-opposite of the speech. Both passages are very nearly of the same length, and seem to be subdivided into three movements which run somewhat parallel. But where the speech proceeds from the slayer to the slain, and from the royal victim to the queenly mourner, the soliloquy moves from that suggestive figure to another king and finally toward another villain. And where the speech leads from action to passion, the soliloquy reverses this direction. Where the Player's diction is heavily external, underlining the fundamental discrepancy between words and deeds, Hamlet's words are by convention his thoughts, directing inward their jabs of self-accusation. Midway, where the Player curses Fortune as a strumpet, Hamlet falls "a-cursing like a very drab." Well may he hesitate, "like a neutral to his will and matter," at the very point where even the rugged Pyrrhus paused and did nothing. Though we need not go so far as Racine, who refined that model of bloody retribution into the gallant lover of Andromaque ("*violent mais sincère*"), we may cite the precedent as a justification—if further justification still be needed—for Hamlet's often criticized delay. While he must hold his tongue, so long as he "cannot speak" his genuine sentiments, the Player is vocal on his behalf. Since he is all too literally "the observed of all observers," he must enact a comedy and so must they: the courtly comedy of fashionable observance. He offers Rosencrantz and Guildenstern the same treatment that he accords the Players, to whom he also must "show fairly outwards." Polonius, who has acted in his youth, ends—all too ironically—as Hamlet's "audience." And while the courtiers watch Hamlet, he watches Claudius, the most subtle impersonator of them all, who conceals his villainy behind a smile and only reveals it while watching a dramatic performance.

Afterwards, when Hamlet confronts his mother with her "act," he undertakes to show her "a glass / Where you may see the inmost part of you." The Elizabethan conception of art as the glass of nature was ethical rather than realistic; for it assumed that, by contemplating situations which reflected their own, men and women could mend their ways and act with greater resolution thereafter. To the observer who is painfully learning the distinction between *seems* and *is,* the hideous pangs of the Trojan Queen are the mirrored distortions of Gertrude's regal insincerities. The "damn'd defeat" of Priam, reminding Hamlet of his father, prompts him to renounce his hitherto passive role, to soliloquize on the Player's example, and finally to evolve his plan of action. Thus his soliloquy departs from, and returns to, the theatrical sphere. "The play's the thing"—the play-within-the-play, where the Player's "passionate speech" will be crowned by the Play Queen's "passionate action," and the crime will be metaphorically ("tropically") re-enacted, beginning and ending with Hamlet's echoed quotations from two notorious tragedies of revenge. Meanwhile the situation at hand is transcended by the searching question in Hamlet's mind—a question which ponders not only the technique of acting, but the actual nature of the esthetic process. Why should the Player—"Tears in his eyes, distraction in's aspect"—have been carried away by the speech? Was he, like the Platonic rhapsode, literally inspired?

Did he feel the part because he was well trained in what today would be known as the Stanislavsky method? Or would he sustain the paradox, which French philosophers have argued, that the most moving actor is the most cold-blooded hypocrite?

> What's Hecuba to him, or he to Hecuba,
> That he should weep for her?

What is the relationship of the player to the play, of the dancer to the dance, of the work of art to its interpretation, or of the interpreter to the audience? How, Shakespeare asks himself in effect, can emotion be communicated by my dramaturgy?

Observe—and here I beg leave to reduce our text for the moment to a paradigm (see page 41)—that he does not present Hecuba's emotions directly. Her passion, unlike Thisbe's, is neither presented nor described. Instead he describes her appearance and appeals to the spectator: "Who, O who," he opines—or even more lugubriously, as the Quartos would have it. "Who, ah woe!"—whoever viewed that spectacle would repudiate destiny itself. Thence the poet appeals the case to a higher court:

> But if the gods themselves did *see* her, then,
> When she [Hecuba] *saw* Pyrrhus make malicious sport,
> In mincing with his sword her husband's [Priam's] limbs—

even they (the GODS) might feel an emotional response, though such a prospect is conditionally stated. Let us meet the condition by recognizing their existence on a highly figurative plane, and by characterizing their attitude as *compassion:* a sympathetic participation in the feelings of Hecuba. They are not besought, as in *King Lear* (II.iv.275–81), to instill a vengeful animus. When Claudius subsequently hints at his devious purposes, Hamlet retorts that these are known to heaven: "I see a cherub that sees them." An ultimate vision is glimpsed as indirectly as the flicker on the wall of Plato's cave. The same double process of visualization and recognition works toward a different end, when Hamlet sees Claudius see the play. When Ophelia expresses Hamlet's plight and her own, she sums it up in a couplet which is her version of his "O cursed spite!"

> O woe is me
> T' have seen what I have seen, see what I see!

Laertes, when he sees Ophelia's madness, will call the gods to witness; and Gertrude will be the witness—or, at all events, the choric narrator—of Ophelia's death. HECUBA is likewise an onlooker, tense though the bond of sympathy must be that unites her to the agonies of Priam; it is he who feels, who suffers physically when Pyrrhus acts. PYRRHUS is your man of *action*, in the most epical and

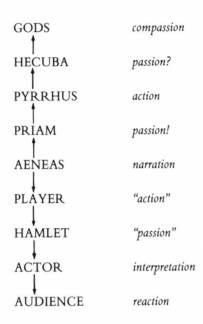

GODS	*compassion*
↑	
HECUBA	*passion?*
↑	
PYRRHUS	*action*
↑	
PRIAM	*passion!*
↑	
AENEAS	*narration*
↓	
PLAYER	*"action"*
↓	
HAMLET	*"passion"*
↓	
ACTOR	*interpretation*
↓	
AUDIENCE	*reaction*

extroverted signification of the term: the key to this passage is the emphasis that Shakespeare places upon his insensibility. Furthermore, no effort is made to present the sufferings of PRIAM: his falling city sympathizes with him, his animistic sword rebels against him, but he himself remains inanimate. Tradition depicts him slain upon the altar of Apollo, and—although Shakespeare makes no point of this circumstance—it sheds the light of religious ritual upon his sacrifice, and helps to explain why so many generations could identify it with their experience. In terms of sheer brutality, or ritualistic fulfilment, the murder might be regarded as a *passion,* and differentiated by an exclamation-point from the question-mark that might appropriately designate the psychological *passion* of Hecuba. But even the burden of her grief, as we have noticed, is relayed to higher authorities: if the gods exist and look down, perhaps their compassionate overview will gather up the vicarious passions of the dead Priam, the unfeeling Pyrrhus, and the muffled queen. And we are left confronting a dizzying hierarchy of externalized emotion, which continues to refer our query upwards until it is out of sight.

Let us therefore look in the other direction, downwards—from the eyes of the gods, past Hecuba and the murderer and the murdered, to the voice of the narrator. When all is said and done, we must not forget that it is AENEAS who speaks: a surviving eye-witness who relives the tale as he tells it to Dido. Since she is not represented, its impact on her goes unregistered. But since the epic has been adapted to the drama, *narration* has become *action* in quotation-marks, simulated actuality; while Aeneas is enacted by the PLAYER. Shakespeare exploits the ambiguity of the verb "to act," which alternates between "doing" and "seeming," between the brutal deeds of Pyrrhus and the verbal hypocrisies that Hamlet dwells on: "For they are actions that a man might play." By means of his acting, the Player simulates *passion,* again in quotation-marks; he functions as a surrogate for the various mythical figures whose respective sorrows he personifies, and bridges the gap between their world and Hamlet's. David Garrick, as HAMLET, attempted to strengthen this understanding between them by the dubious business of pantomiming the Player's words. The scene's effectiveness depends precisely upon the differentiation between their passive and active roles. The Player need not "tear a passion to tatters," but neither should he be "too tame," and under latter-day stage direction he is likelier to err by domesticating verse into drawing-room prose. Simply to "suit the action to the words" is, in this instance, to be something of a Termagant. And who could be histrionic with better right than a Shakespearean actor acting an actor? Hamlet's expressed distrust of histrionics, on the other hand, lends an air of naturalness to his own behavior: hence, according to Partridge in *Tom Jones,* Garrick as Hamlet is not much of an actor, while anybody may see that the King is really acting. Furthermore, this natural Hamlet must put on an "antic disposition," must from time to time assume a mask of madness which derives significance from whatever distinction he manages to establish between his real and his raving selves. Even now, in the constraining presence of Rosencrantz and Guildenstern and Polonius, he has started to rehearse. And the Hamlet who consequently emerges from inaction can — and on occasion does — out-Herod the players, challenging Laertes to mouth and rant in the vein of *Hercules Furens,* and recounting his sea-adventure as if it were a play. Within a few years his name will already become such a byword for theatricalism that, in a poem on *The Passion of Love* by Anthony Scoloker, the lover "Calls Players fooles . . . Will learn them Action . . . Much like mad-*Hamlet;* thus a Passion teares."

Since the theater perforce exaggerates, amplifying its pathos and stylizing its diction, it takes a specially marked degree of amplification and stylization to dramatize the theatrical, as Schlegel realized. Conversely, when matters pertaining to the stage are exhibited upon the stage, to acknowledge their artificiality is to enhance the realism of everything else within view. The contrasting textures of the Player's fustian and Hamlet's lines, like the structural contrast between the prevailing blank verse and the rhyming couplets of the play-within-the-play, bring out the realities of the situation by exposing its theatricalities. By exaggeration of drama, by "smelling a little too strongly of the buskin" in Dryden's phrase, Shakespeare achieves his imitation of life. Yet the play itself — not "The Murder of Gonzago" but *The Tragedy of Hamlet, Prince of Denmark* — is "a fiction," an illusion which we accept on poetic faith. Hamlet's passion is sincere and sentient as compared to the Player's which—though externalized and factitious—has aroused Hamlet from passivity to action. And of course he is not, in the very last analysis, "passion's slave"; he is, he becomes, an agent of revenge; he suits "the word to the action." Nor is he a recorder to be played upon, though he succeeds in playing upon Claudius. The implied comparison with Aeneas would be completed by Dido's counterpart in the neglected person of Ophelia, but dalliance in either case is resolutely cut off. When Hamlet hits upon his ingenious plot, it projects him in two directions at once: back to the plane of intradramatic theatricals, and forward to the plane of his audience. A spectator of the players, he has his own spectators, who turn out to be ourselves, to whom he is actually an ACTOR. Here we stand in relation to him—that is, to his interpreter, be he Garrick or Gielgud—where he stands in relation to the Player. The original emotion, having been handed down from one level to another of metaphor and myth and impersonation and projection, reaches the basic level of *interpretation,* whence the expression can make its impression upon our minds. There the reality lodges, in the *reaction* of the AUDIENCE: the empathy that links our outlook with a chain of being which sooner or later extends all the way from the actors to the gods.

Shakespeare's appeal to his audience, like Orlando's to the Duke Senior in *As You Like It* (II.vii.117), is always made on the basis of common experience: if we are expected to sympathize, it is because we "know what 'tis to pity and be pitied." On the dramatist's side, his insight into character—which the eighteenth century termed "sympathetic imagination"—is concretely based upon his ability to enter into many different lives and to respond, vicariously yet whole-heartedly, to all the situations they encounter. If tragedy induces pity and fear, we must also remember that Aristotle defined pity as fear lest the fate of others overtake ourselves. Asking us to put ourselves in Hamlet's—or Hecuba's—place, Shakespeare stages a series of emotional displacements all along the line. His willingness to share her unhappiness, across so many removes, and even to question the ways of providence as manifested toward her, finds its polar opposite in the fable of La Fontaine (X.13), where the object-lesson is viewed in relatively comfortable detachment:

> Quiconcque, en pareil cas, se croit haï des Cieux,
> Qu'il considère Hécube; il rendra grâce aux dieux.

[Whoever, in any such case, believes himself hated by Heaven,
Let him consider Hecuba; he will give thanks to the gods.]

That remote Hecuba, the *ne plus ultra of* of misfortune, and therefore a properly qualified exemplar of the consolations of philosophy, is still significant, still archetypal within the literary frame of reference. The failure of modern literature to maintain a relationship with her and what she represents is the failure of modern life to sustain human relationships, as Aldous Huxley interprets them in *Antic Hay*. There, to the syncopated rhythm of the foxtrot and the modulated timbre of the saxophone, our Shakespearean theme is given what may well be a final variation:

> What's he to Hecuba?
> Nothing at all.
> That's why there'll be no wedding on Wednesday week,
> Way down in old Bengal.

The marriage of minds, as Shakespeare arranges it, admits fewer impediments. If now and then it turns actors into virtual spectators, there are reciprocal occasions on which the spectators are virtually turned into actors. When Hamlet, glancing excitedly in three directions, says:

> I have heard
> That guilty creatures, sitting at a play,
> Have by the very cunning of the scene
> Been struck

we shift in our seats uneasily, wondering whether there may not be a Claudius in the house. Audience-participation engenders what might be termed a play-outside-the-play. It is hard to see how Shakespeare's original Gravedigger, speaking of Hamlet's voyage to England, could have kept from winking at the English groundlings when he said: "There the men are as mad as he." Elizabethan drama is full of such interplay between the stage and the pit, as well as the tiring-house. Playwrights were not less conscious of their medium than Pirandello or Tieck. For Shakespeare, whose world was a stage and whose theater was the Globe, life itself could be "a poor player," the best of actors could be "but shadows," and Hamlet's ambition could be "the shadow of a dream." Of the roles that the playwright may have played himself, we hear of two in particular, one of them the Ghost in *Hamlet*. It has been traditional for the actor who plays that role to double as the First Player. May we not suppose, without straining conjecture very far, that it was Shakespeare who first delivered the Player's speech; and that he is speaking expressly, through its rhetorical configurations, of how poetry accomplishes its effects?

Acts III and IV:
Problems of Text and Staging

Ruth Nevo

In the volume of commentary upon the most famous of all soliloquies, one salient fact is often overlooked: that it occurs at the outset of Act III, the act which contains the *processus turbarum* [the perturbations and dangers classically a feature of the crisis phase of tragedy] and brings the action to a turning point. Contrivance, conspiracy, concealment, and dissimulation reach their crisis in the sequence that runs from the nunnery scene through the play scene to the killing of Polonius behind the arras. This sequence articulates the peripeteia—the complete reversal of Hamlet's situation. He who was Denmark's honored prince (and is still, after all, heir apparent) becomes in the eyes of all an overt menace to the kingdom, and this fact is exploited by Claudius, who seizes the opportunity to rid himself of his dangerous nephew. The inner progress of Hamlet through this chapter of perturbations is the progress toward a great frustration: a blind alley where both knowledge and freedom are totally confounded, and all planning brought to nought.

It is as a point upon this inner progress that the third soliloquy can most profitably be viewed. A general impression of the speech as expressing again that disaffection with life with which the play opened raises no problems. The Ghost's revelation, the duplicity of Rosencrantz and Guildenstern, Ophelia's pitiable helplessness to sustain him in his growing suspicion of all who surround him in Claudius' court, his own experience of suspense and uncertainty are sufficient to account for a melancholy acute enough to make life wearisome and the sleep of death appealing. Moreover, the strongly ethical bent of Hamlet's nature expresses itself naturally in the questioning of values and the weighing of options which

From *Tragic Form in Shakespeare.* © 1972 by Princeton University Press. Originally entitled "Hamlet."

form the speech's content. Its catalogue of adversities has often enough been noticed to have little relevance to Hamlet's specific situation, but an outgoing of sympathy, a partisanship with humankind is, as Sewall has noted, a characteristic consequence of the tragic hero's own distress. Again, while the speech appears to backtrack upon Hamlet's immediately preceding decision to stage the Mousetrap and catch the conscience of the King, the opposition between active and passive modes of response links it with its predecessor in a quite specific way. Endurance, suffering in the mind, the absorption of adversity, corresponds to Hecuba; the taking of arms against a sea of troubles and by opposing ending them, to Pyrrhus.

The critical problem arises from the perception that the speech apparently confuses two issues. Since we know what Hamlet's obligatory task is, we cannot but register the possibility that the taking of arms and the "enterprises of great pitch and moment" refer to the killing of Claudius, though the logic of the syntax makes them refer to the self-slaughter which is the subject of the whole disquisition. And conversely, because self-slaughter is the ostensible subject of the whole disquisition, we cannot read the speech simply as a case of conscience in the matter of revenge — Christian conscience producing impediments to the action dictated by the code of revenge and the secular sanctions and motivations of honor. Whether Hamlet is talking of his revenge or of his desire for death, or of both, one substituting for the other as mask for truth (or truth for mask) therefore becomes the problem that this speech poses. It is customary again to invoke depth psychology and the strategies of rationalization for a solution to this crux. But the dramatic critic, I would suggest, should anchor his interpretations in drama's method of progression by thrust and counterthrust rather than in the causal axioms of psychology. The speech is a reaction from the determination which ended the "rogue and peasant slave" soliloquy. It is not a cause of this reaction that we should attempt to uncover — such reactions are a fact of emotional life, and causes for melancholy he has in plenty — but the effects it functions to produce: the further disclosures and discoveries which it proffers us.

In the Quarto of 1603 the speech precedes the previous scene of the players, as indeed does the whole of the nunnery scene, and it is occasioned very plausibly. It evidently represents Hamlet's reflections upon the content of the book Polonius notices him reading as he sets his trap for Ophelia in order to discover the cause of the prince's distemper. In the First Quarto the speech is purely a reflection upon suicide by the grief-stricken, melancholy-mad Hamlet (much madder in the First Quarto than in the later versions), in which neither the lines "Whether 'tis nobler in the mind to suffer" nor "And enterprises of great pitch and moment" appear. There is thus no possibility of reference to the matter of revenge at all. "Conscience" makes cowards of us all in the First Quarto too, but it is, significantly, the "hope" not the dread of something after death which

"pusles the braine, and doth confound the sence,⌉
Which makes us rather beare those evilles we have,
Than flie to others that we know not of."

If in the debate upon the provenance of the Bad Quarto we take the side of those who see it as a preliminary (mutilated) draft of the play as we have it from the Second Quarto and Folio, rather than as a garbled copy or a shorthand record of a performance of the longer and better version, I believe we can throw considerable (if speculative) light upon the "To be" speech, and suggest the direction in which it is to be taken. For it was surely the keen shaping sense of an assured artistry that exchanged the First Quarto equivalent of Act II for the brilliant and subtle and technically extremely original dramatization of the player scene, with its dynamic projection of a finely conceived dilemma, and reserved the nunnery scene (which has no bearing upon the main revenge action) for the confusions and perturbations of Act III. The "To be" speech, transferred along with the nunnery scene, is now no simple dialogue of self and soul upon the question of suicide but a much more complex reflection. The speech articulates Hamlet's heartsick realization of what is involved in the act of choice: its insuperable difficulties and the price to be paid by him who would be elector of himself. This is exactly the import and the effect of the two interpolations:

> Whether 'tis nobler in the mind to suffer
> The slings and arrows of outrageous fortune,
> Or to take arms against a sea of troubles,
> And by opposing end them?

and

> And enterprises of great pitch and moment
> With this regard their currents turn awry
> And lose the name of action.

The complexity which is thus added to the cruder figure of the First Quarto complicates, of course, the critic's exegetical task. So radically ambiguous in import has the speech become, while at the same time so readily detachable, so generalized and therefore applicable to a host of occasions for melancholy reflections upon adversity, that Lamb's despair is understandable indeed: "I confess myself," he says,

> utterly unable to appreciate that celebrated speech . . . or to tell whether it be good, bad or indifferent; it has been so handled and pawed about by declamatory boys and men, and torn so inhumanly from its living place and principle of continuity in the play, till it has become to me a perfect dead member.

Nevertheless it has a "living place and principle of continuity": its position in Act III. It is this positioning that can direct the emphasis to fall upon the bafflement that the speech expresses rather than upon the sense of a dilemma which it also (however obscurely) suggests. Choice of action, Hamlet is saying, depends upon knowledge that is simply not available to the human mind. Hamlet's very syntax enacts the inextricable entanglement of cognition with volition, the "puzzling" of the "will." The bare, unmodified infinitive — "to be" — suggests a hovering upon the brink of an act. Yet the following lines introduce a question of preliminary knowledge — or judgment — of what is noble. What Hamlet is recognizing as the conscience which makes him a coward and causes action to lose its name subsumes and transcends the conflict of philosophy with religion, or of duty with desire. Hamlet's pale case of thought is precisely what it says it is — that mental activity which counters every option with its opposite, every consideration with its contrary; which takes in aspects and calculates consequences; which is stilled only by and in action, but which makes every choice of action seemingly impossible. From this cul-de-sac he sees no escape. His thought moves in clogged and wearisome circles, for he cannot know the answer to the question that he asks. Neither instinct nor ratiocination can endow value with certainty, and therefore freedom and virtue themselves are a snare and a delusion. Hamlet expresses the depth of his dismay at this discovery, which is, at some time, every thinking being's discovery. That it is so is the secret of the speech's immense popularity.

It is to further and more searing recognitions of the limitations of mind that the whole of the third act is directed. For the third act presents, with an unparalleled wealth of resource, the confounding of knowledge with knowledge and the futility of passion and action.

I take the subdued and abstracted "Nymph, in thy orisons / Be all my sins remember'd" (III.i.89–90) as Johnson did, to be "grave and solemn," and not accusatory and sarcastic. Hamlet has hardly yet emerged from the intense preoccupation of the soliloquy. But from the moment he is jerked to attention by the gauche little importunity of Ophelia's return of his gifts to the end of his tirade, the scene becomes a powerful image of the inscrutability of appearances. The fact that the audience is informed of the "espials" of Polonius and the King while Hamlet is not permits the nunnery scene to dramatize the impenetrability and duplicity of appearance in the most direct and unequivocal mode of dramatic irony — that which obtains when the audience is in possession of more information than either the protagonist or the watchers behind the arras. All parties to the scene are on the watch. The audience watches the two spies watching Hamlet, speculating upon his motives and behavior; the audience watches Hamlet probing the genuineness of Ophelia's feelings, and announcing his own with wildly contradictory declarations, the degree of the sincerity of which it has no means of knowing; and the audience watches Ophelia utterly bewildered by all she sees and hears, and hiding in her heart the knowledge of her own role as decoy. The ellipses of Hamlet's speech force the audience to its own speculations, chief among them the question whether Hamlet knows or discovers the presence of Polonius and the King. Few can fail to have been beguiled at some time by Dover Wilson's proposal of a lost stage direction at II.ii.162, which would allow Hamlet, reading on his book, to enter in time to overhear "I'll loose my daughter to him"; or for that matter by the older stage tradition which makes Polonius betray his presence by an inadvertent movement. (I count myself gratefully among the many who were bewitched [and am on record to this effect in a published article of some years ago], but have since come to believe that a rendering of the scene based upon the pun [at any of several possible points] and Hamlet's previous overhearing of Polonius, require a sleight-of-hand ingenuity which must be beyond the capacity of acting to convey. Powerful recent support for this view is to be found in the closely reasoned and admirably concise argument of H. Jenkins against the invocation of either pun or earlier entrance. "I suspect," he concludes, that "when the nunnery, at whatever stage, becomes a brothel, it becomes a red herring"; and he points out that "what the play requires is not that Hamlet shall know but that we shall know, that the King is there to hear.") But it should be noted that we actually need no further explanation for Hamlet's sudden "Where's your father?" than the fact that he has not recently been permitted her presence unchaperoned, if at all. And his apparent change of mood at that point in the scene might well be attributed to recollected angry resentment at Polonius' interference in his affairs. Indeed, this would seem to be born out by the diatribe on calumny — he being calumniated and exposed by his courtship of Ophelia to the insulting aspersions of such as Polonius.

I am inclined to believe that the deeper dramatic purport of the scene is obscured if Hamlet is made or becomes aware of Polonius at any point in the scene. For if Hamlet knows that Polonius is behind the arras, then he knows that Ophelia is lying when she tells him her father is at home — knows, therefore, that she is deceiving him. Whereas it is precisely his total inability to know her, or for that matter himself, that the scene, in this theatrically simpler view, would allow us to perceive as the center of his anguish. He is tormented precisely by doubts, not by confirmations. And how indeed should he know what Ophelia is? Is she loving and faithful to him despite parental authority? Or compliant to the latter and therefore false to him? What has she been told about him? Is he not testing her with his hyperbolic declaration:

> I am very proud, revengeful, ambitious; with more offenses at my
> back than I have thoughts to put them in, imagination to give them
> shape, or time to act them in?

His mother has predisposed him to believe in women's perfidy, has produced in him a revulsion from sex and the stratagems of sex; he was unable to draw Ophelia's face by his perusal; she has refused his letters and denied him access; now she returns his gifts. What form of devious double-dealing shall he expect? He is wary, defensive. Yet he did love her once and is enraged by the thought of the father's meddling. It is surely an extremity of ambivalence that is expressed in the violent paradoxes of

> If thou dost marry, I'll give thee this plague for thy dowry. Be thou as chaste as ice, as pure as snow, thou shalt not escape calumny. Get thee to a nunnery, go: farewell. Or, if thou wilt needs marry, marry a fool; for wise men know well enough what monsters you make of them.
>
> (III.i.135–39)

It is not absolutely necessary to take "those that are married already, all but one, shall live; the rest shall keep as they are" as an overt threat to the King behind the arras, for Hamlet could be thus obliquely discharging his bosom of the perilous stuff, which is, after all, the root cause of all his agitations; and doing so in a semi-aside to the *audience,* who will then wonder what the King will make of it. The scene culminates in the tirade against false faces and the ape-like antics of a lying world, generalized by the "you," which takes the place of the previous intimate "thou":

> God has given you one face, and you make yourselves another; you jig, you amble, and you lisp, and nickname God's creatures, and make your wantonness your ignorance.
>
> (III.i.149–53)

This is the familiar Renaissance complaint against cosmetics, against appearance and masked intention. But his final "Get thee to a nunnery" implies again sufficient tenderness for Ophelia to wish her preserved from corruption. The scene in its ambivalence and consternation accumulates a powerful charge of disgust with all the grotesque iniquities of the world as well as those of women.

In the play scene Hamlet stages his grand exposure of these iniquities. And it is in this sequence that his intention, the triumphant revealing of reality behind appearances, the peeling of the skin of hypocrisy from the onion of truth, will be at once achieved and frustrated in the play's central reversal. Hamlet's instructions to the players reflect his sense of his own aim and aspiraton:

> for in the very torrent, tempest, and, as I may say, the whirlwind of passion, you must acquire and beget a temperance that may give it

smoothness. Oh, it offends me to the soul, to hear a robustious peri-
wig-pated fellow tear a passion to tatters, to very rags, to split the
ears of the groundlings.

(III.ii.6–13)

Passion is the powerhouse of the soul, the generator of all deeds. But control of
passion is above all requisite for any effective expression or action. Without such
temperance a man is no more than passion's slave. His encomium to Horatio
directly expresses his desire for that stoic impassivity in the face of fortune's buffets and rewards that he admires in his friend in the degree that he has found it
wanting in himself.

It is thus mastery of passion and of circumstance that Hamlet enacts in the
play scene. *Régisseur* prince, as Fergusson has called him, with his fiction of the
players he holds the mirror up to nature; he will reveal the inner truth of the guilty
creatures sitting at the play. He will expose their real faces. The fiction will reflect their truth, making the mask drop from them. The assumed role of the
Player King will expose the assumed virtue of the hypocrite King. Not only the
King's conscience will be caught, but also the Queen's. Hence his interpolated
jibes: "No, good mother, here's metal more attractive"; "look you, how cheer-
fully my mother looks"; "O, but she'll keep her word," "Wormwood, wormwood." In order to wound his mother he makes Ophelia her proxy, treating her
like a harlot, with deliberate and brutal sexual contempt, forcing their dialogue
of innuendos to bear the worst constructions. Meantime he masks his own truth
with his riddling talk of ambition, crammed capons, and the chameleon's dish
(knowing how easily motives of thwarted ambition will be imputed to him), and
introduces a puzzling hidden threat into the already enigmatic situation for the
benefit of the court, which hears him announce that Lucianus is nephew to the
King.

The audience, again watching the watcher being watched, is drawn into the
tissue of guesswork, speculation, and inference out of which the scene is made.
All are in the dark — the court audience ignorant, Hamlet in suspense; and Hamlet's sore distraction has never seemed more open and palpable to his fellows.

Since the dumb show draws no response, the audience itself is put into the
same suspense. I believe Shakespeare's stagecraft here to be both more crude and
more profound than Dover Wilson's marvel of ingenuity, which takes more
subtlety to follow than any audience can be assumed to have possessed. An Elizabethan audience, or perhaps any other, is likely to be undisturbed by the King's
apparent inconsistency of response. It will not have supposed for a moment that
an accomplished courtier would give himself away at the first hint of danger,
more particularly as the essence of his quandary is his ignorance of what, or how

much, Hamlet knows. It is after all a war of nerves between him and Hamlet; if his nerves are strong enough for a great deal but no more, so much the more plausible the entire episode.

The King breaks down; Hamlet has triumphed. He has made the galled jade wince and the truth unkennel itself. It is his text that the players, the court, the King, and the Queen all play. He is master of reality, making his will prevail, no fool of fortune. His elation is unbounded; and superbly expressed in the scene with Horatio which follows the Mousetrap, and in the cloud scene with Polonius, where he fools those who would fool him, articulating through the metaphors of recorders' stops and cloud-shapes his own inscrutable willful mastery. But his will, now at the top of its bent, has its crucial tests before it.

In the prayer scene and the closet scene his devices are overthrown. His mastery is confounded by the inherent liability of human reason to jump to conclusions, to fail to distinguish seeming from being. He, of all people, is trapped in the fatal deceptive maze of appearances that is the phenomenal world. Never perhaps has the mind's finitude been better dramatized than in the prayer scene and in the closet scene. Another motto of the Player King is marvelously fulfilled in the nexus of ironies which constitutes the play's peripeteia: "Our thoughts are ours, their ends none of our own." In the sequence of events following Hamlet's elation at the success of the Mousetrap, and culminating in the death of Polonius, all things are the opposite of what they seem, and action achieves the reverse of what was intended. Here in the play's peripeteia is enacted Hamlet's fatal error, his fatal misjudgment, which constitutes the crisis of the action, and is the directly precipitating cause of his own death, seven other deaths, and Ophelia's madness.

When the opportunity for his revenge offers itself and is not taken, the reason is given with the greatest explicitness:

> Now might I do it pat, now he is praying;
> And now I'll do't; and so he goes to Heaven;
> And so am I revenged. That would be scann'd:
> A villain kills my father; and for that,
> I, his sole son, do this same villain send
> To heaven.
> Oh, this is hire and salary, not revenge.
> He took my father grossly, full of bread,
> With all his crimes broad blown, as flush as May;
> And how his audit stands who knows save heaven:
> But in our circumstance and course of thought
> 'Tis heavy with him; and am I then revenged,
> To take him in the purging of his soul,

When he is fit and season'd for his passage?
No.
Up, sword, and know thou a more horrid hent;
When he is drunk asleep, or in his rage,
Or in the incestuous pleasure of his bed,
At gaming, swearing, or about some act
That has no relish of salvation in't;
Then trip him, that his heels may kick at heaven,
And that his soul may be as damn'd and black
As hell, whereto it goes.

(III.iii.73–95)

Hamlet spares the King at prayer not because the King is a suppliant and helpless figure; nor, certainly, because "Vengeance is mine, saith the Lord"; nor merely out of an excessive and savage vindictiveness. Hamlet spares the King in his moment of prayer out of his need not merely for good reasons for action but for the best reasons; for total consonance between deed and retribution. Less than an absolute justice will not denote him truly, will not gain the assent of his inmost soul. Nothing less than the fittingness of punishment to crime can assuage the pain of his constant knowledge, so recently confirmed, of the lying, smiling humbug of the King's evil. Only so can he justify himself in his own eyes. Only a manifestation of divine justice in its perfection can express and appease his abhorrence and set his spirit at rest. But the elder Hamlet's spirit did not demand this of him. Nor is it demanded of any man. He plays providence, and the distinction that marked him out as tragic hero — the high demand for absolute truth shining forth in appearances — becomes corrupted in that moment of hubris by the taint of a fatal aestheticism. He becomes the artist caught in the love of his own devices, and sacrifices the deed — the end — which is the moral imperative of his situation, upon the altar of the aesthetically satisfying means.

That it is appearances that deceive him is of the essence of the irony. For the King in fact is not in a state of grace at all, and Hamlet's reasoning is based on false premises, false appearances, both when he believes the praying King to be purging his soul, and so spares him, and when he believes Polonius to be the spying King, and so kills him. The Jacobean avenger is in the nature of things a complex figure — judge and executioner, victim and culprit at once; mediating between divinely absolute and humanly contingent justice. Vendice too is hoist with his own petard in an access of overweening pride in his accomplishments as artist of revenge. The *Revenger's Tragedy* followed *Hamlet,* and throws into bold relief what was implicit in the earlier play where Hamlet's hubris represents a far subtler and more daring conception of this perfectionism. The symbolic action in which he exhibits it—the staging of the Mousetrap and its aftermath—indicates the presence of one of Shakespeare's major preoccupations: the power of the artist's will to master reality is a theme that takes many forms in many plays, and receives its final wry exorcism when Prospero—*régisseur* magician—drowns his book at the end of the *Tempest*.

Hamlet's production, at all events, is a failure. What Hamlet does do is as fatally erroneous as what he does not do; the premeditated action that he does not take is as fraught with evil consequences as the unpremeditated action that he does take. The good that he would do he does not, and the evil that he would not do he does. He exemplifies, without knowing it, the condition Claudius, ahead of him, knows so well:

> O limed soul, that struggling to be free,
> Art more engaged!
>   (III.iii.68–69)

The avenger, the thunderbearer, who could drink hot blood in the fierce joy of his resolution and his certain knowledge of the King's guilt, not only fails to dispatch the evildoer, but instead murders an innocent man. Now he bears not only a tainted mind but a bloodstained hand; is involved irrevocably in the evil he fought; and has never been further from his task, or more infirm of purpose.

In the closet scene, where Hamlet is intent upon moving his mother to see, as in a glass, the inmost part of her, to see as he sees and so to admit the enormity of what she has done, a further ironic reversal of expectation is brought about. For he is as mistaken about Gertrude as he was mistaken about Ophelia. She is not, on any evidence that the text provides, the murderer of her husband, nor a party to the murder. Her comment on the protesting lady revealed no more, it seems, than a worldly self-possession. It is Hamlet's delusion that is manifested in the closet scene. "Look here, upon this picture, and on this," he demands. How could you leave to feed on this fair mountain and batten on this moor? Have you eyes? Can you not *see* a paddock, a bat, a gib? What I believe should now be realized to the full is that, in very truth, she cannot see. Nor could the audience, who has seen what she has seen: a suave and polished courtier, of plausive manner and smiling mien. To Hamlet it is by now self-evident that this is a satyr, a mildewed ear, a king of shreds and patches, but he is in this deluded. It is not self-evident at all. There is no mark of Cain upon the murderer's forehead. There is no art by which we can find the mind's construction in the face.

It is to be remarked how insistently Hamlet throws the emphasis of his castigation upon what he sees as an error of judgment qua judgment:

> You cannot call it love, for at your age
> The hey-day in the blood is tame, it's humble,

> And waits upon the judgment; and what judgment
> Would step from this to this? Sense sure you have,
> Else could you not have motion; but sure, that sense
> Is apoplex'd, for madness would not err,
> Nor sense to ecstasy was ne'er so thrall'd
> But it reserved some quantity of choice,
> To serve in such a difference. What devil was't
> That thus hath cozen'd you at hoodman-blind?
>
> (III.iv.68–77)

The wheel has come full circle, and opaque and inscrutable appearances seem now to be transparent to Hamlet. But they are not, as his own recent blindness ironically underlines. The closet scene with its arras, its images, and its apparition, is a Shakespearean equivalent of the Platonic parable of the cave. Shadow and substance, image, conception, apparition, illusion, play a baffling blindman's buff. Never was Donne's "Poor soul, in this thy flesh what doest thou know?" better illustrated; nor dramatic irony denser than in Gertrude's answer to Hamlet's "Do you see nothing there?": "Nothing at all; yet all that is I see." In these great central scenes of the play Hamlet's downfall enacts the epistemological anxiety of the age. Montaigne's dictum that the plague of man is the presumption of knowledge and Donne's scorn of the "Pedantery, / Of being taught by sense, and fantasie," here acquire an unexampled resonance.

Hamlet's own recognition of fallibility emerges at the close of the closet scene. By the time he has (mistakenly) spared the King, and mistakenly killed Polonius; by the time, chastened by the Ghost, he has acknowledged his blunted purposes and has found it in his heart to ask his mother to "assume a virtue, if you have it not," it has become clear, with the brutal clarity of irony, that it is indeed only in the counterfeit presentment of the playhouse, or in the mind of God, that the word can be made flesh or truth transparent in appearance. "Forgive me this my virtue" is his striking expression of a new humility. "Assume a virtue, if you have it not" is a very minimal demand for the arrogant and accusatory young man of the first act who announced that he knew not "seems."

The death of Polonius, hated and despised as he was, calls forth in Hamlet an awareness of a common tragic destiny. And this common tragic destiny he sees under the aspect of a providence at work behind the appearances of chance:

> heaven hath pleased it so,
> To punish me with this, and this with me,
> That I must be their scourge and minister
>
> (III.iv.173–75)

Nevertheless, in what can be interpreted as a reflex of pride, of self-assertive rebellion against that shared destiny, that shared instrumentality, he later in the same scene grimly rejoices at the prospect of counterintrigue, and concludes with the deliberate obscenity of "I'll lug the guts into the neighbor room," whereby he would make his victim, if he could, a distant and indifferent object.

Since both the Folio and the Quartos are silent upon the matter of act division after II.ii, the delimitation of Act IV has remained a vexed question. Johnson found "this modern division into Acts" (at IV.i of the accepted text) "not very happy, for the pause is made at a time when there is more continuity of action than in almost any other of the scenes." This is at the point immediately after the closet scene, when the Queen is conveying to Claudius the substance of her conclusions that Hamlet is "mad as the sea and wind." The murder of Polonius is discovered, and Rosencrantz and Guildenstern are dispatched to find Hamlet, who confuses his interlocutors with riddling remarks about the location of Polonius — "in heaven," or possibly "i' the other place," but at all events where "he will stay till ye come." The three short scenes possess an obvious continuity. There would seem to be no reason whatever, in view of the fluidity and continuity of Elizabethan stage practice, to have the act division at that point. Several nineteenth-century commentators concurred with Johnson's opinion that the act division should logically be made at IV.iv, where Fortinbras enters upon his expedition and Hamlet is on his way to England. This scene was cut in the Folio with the approval of several later critics. Lloyd, for instance, says,

> Beautiful as the soliloquy in this scene is, I am disposed to think that the excision of it may have been deliberate — as unnecessary, prolonging the action, and, it may be, exhibiting the weakness of Hamlet too crudely.

Upon principles derived from the study of Shakespeare's usual practice in the matter of the management of the fourth act, itself developing impressively in skill and subtlety, I believe it possible to perceive and to reconstruct the sequence in such a way as to yield a characteristic and consequential fourth act. There need be little argument concerning the extension of Act III to what is at present IV.iii. This would bring the third act — the culmination of the *processus turbarum,* the reversal of the hero's situation, the disintegration and collapse of his high aims — to a natural close with the rounding-off of the Polonius debacle within the palace of Elsinore. Act IV, "the preparation for the remedy" as the Terentian doctrine had it, must bring Fortinbras into the scope of the play's action, fetch Laertes from Paris upon his sister's death, and begin to engineer to counteraction and hence the catastrophe. In addition to this already weighty task, the old plot demanded that Hamlet be got to sea and back, and that Rosencrantz and Guildenstern be dispatched. Part of the problem Shakespeare solved expeditiously enough, though with inevitable loss of pace and immediacy, by means of the dramatized narration in Hamlet's letter to Horatio and his later retrospective account of the sea voyage. But the sheer difficulty of managing the narrative threads of intrigue, counterintrigue and subintrigue remained formidable. The present act division produces an effect of dislocation and crowding; and a further consequence of the division as we have it is the equally crowded catastrophe of Act V, which is made to contain the gravedigger's comic material (normally found in Shakespeare's fourth acts), Hamlet's leap into the grave, the plotting of Claudius and Laertes, and the complicated duel itself.

Suppose however, that, as has been suggested, Act IV were to begin at IV.iv with Fortinbras, it would then be possible to see the fourth phase as running right through to include the present V.i (the gravediggers and the burial). This would leave, it is true, a shorter Act V, but one in which the whole momentum of the action would be directed to the issue of the duel, with Osric, Character of an Affected Courtier, absurd relic of the painted court, functioning far more effectively than he does at present in an act that is so full of directions as to become obscure in its import. The great virtue of this shift, however, would be to restore Act IV to a form that is recognizably Shakespearean, exhibiting a characteristic control of design, the effect of that sure shaping power which alone can achieve the intelligible spacing and articulating of complex dramatic material.

What we would then have is a fourth act in which the protagonist is brought to the nadir of his tragic progress with the familiar Shakespearean modifying and measuring effects of pathos and irony playing upon him, while the important contrast between the three avenging sons is brought into effective prominence. (A common view taken in the matter of the three avenging sons is that Fortinbras represents an Aristotelean mean or ideal [of honor, virtue, or action], while Hamlet represents defect and Laertes excess. My own view is that the two reflectors of Hamlet serve precisely to bring out the specifically tragic-heroic quality of the protagonist's experience by comparison with their own more commonplace existences. Fortinbras' revenge is a publicly sanctioned matter of armies and alliances [of the kind that is denied Hamlet by virtue of his circumstances]; Laertes', a plunge into the abyss of deception and treachery. Only for Hamlet, who treads the tightrope of the task that is public duty and private burden at once, is his revenge the agent of a tragic self-discovery.) The act would then, in its complex strategy (though not of course in its content) resemble the fourth act of *Lear,* in which despair, pathos, irony, tragic "reunions,"and the comparison between the three victims of adversity—Edgar, Gloucester, and Lear—are all constitutive of the total effect. The act would be consonant with what both the anticipations of previous plays and the developments of later ones leads us to infer as the living principle of Shakespeare's management of his fourth act; and this being so it would allow us to perceive and interpret the episodes with greater confidence. And "How all occasions" need no longer disturb us as unnecessarily prolonging the action, or as showing too crudely the "weakness of Hamlet."

It does indeed represent Hamlet's abdication from what has become the intolerable burden of thought. One continuity is worth noticing. "About, my brain!" (II.ii.627) expressed a determination to enlist thought in the service of action. The "pale cast of thought" (III.i.85) registered his awareness of thought's power to paralyze action. Now in "My thoughts be bloody, or be nothing worth!" Hamlet is willing to subdue thought entirely to blood, to absorb himself in his role of avenger. It is a signal defeat, which we should not, I believe, regard with equanimity. Contemporary experience tells us much about the dangerous violence that can spring from defeated idealistic aspirations, or be released by them. What Hamlet was born (as tragic hero) to discover and to accept is precisely that all occasions do inform against us if we are possessed, and to the degree that we are possessed, of "large discourse"; that the anguish of looking before and after is the price to be paid for the capability and godlike reason which must not fust in us unused. That his own possession of this faculty is at this point subverted and confounded is to be discerned in the very illogic of his soliloquy. In compunction and self-blame he affirms the value of and the need for Fortinbras' uncalculating enterprise, and disparages the "thought" that hinders him, though he is unable to decide whether he thinks too little ("bestial oblivion") or too much ("some craven scruple of thinking too precisely on the event"). If in his despair of solutions he rejects the calculations of the understanding as more perfidious than the oracles, what he enlists as motive and ground for action is now no more than the puff of ambition, the blazon of honor. And in the same breath as he names the ambition of the delicate and tender prince "divine," he exposes its object for what it is — worthless and negligible, an eggshell, a plot that is not tomb enough and continent to hide the slain. Drowning, he clutches at the straw of "greatness," a factitious magnanimity. Man of conscience, of scruples, of considerations and distinctions, he envies Fortinbras his uninhibited sweep of action as he envied the player his uninhibited sweep of expression, as he envied Horatio his power to suffer nothing in suffering all — envied him his freedom from the imperious inner voice which demands integrity, its own inalienably true expression, in acts as in words. Hamlet's problem, the problem of being what he is not, or not being what he is, is here resolved by denial, by a repudiation of his "ordeal of consciousness"; and it is upon this repudiation that Claudius' antiphonal persuasion of Laertes to action — an action which will make him the impulsive tool of Claudius' machinations — throws an ironically revealing and melancholy light:

KING. Laertes, was your father dear to you?
    Or are you like the painting of a sorrow,
    A face without a heart?
LAERTES. Why ask you this?
KING. Not that I think you did not love your father,
    But that I know love is begun by time:
    And that I see, in passages of proof,
    Time qualifies the spark and fire of it;
    There lives within the very flame of love
    A kind of wick or snuff that will abate it;
    And nothing is at a like goodness still,
    For goodness, growing to a plurisy,
    Dies in his own too-much; that we would do
    We should do when we would; for this "would" changes,
    And hath abatements and delays as many,
    As there are tongues, are hands, are accidents;
    And then this "should" is like a spendthrift's sigh,
    That hurts by easing. But to the quick o' the ulcer:
    Hamlet comes back; what would you undertake,
    To show yourself your father's son in deed,
    More than in words?

                          (IV.vii.108–27)

Nothing could bring out with greater force the melancholy perception that the whole play has dramatized. Action traps the actor in the labyrinth of concealed evil: inaction in the toils of time and the lapse of passion.

What in the meantime becomes of human well-being it is the function of Ophelia's madness to reveal. The pathos of the figure, exposed to the pitying gaze of the onlookers, withdrawn into the depths of her lunatic solitude, so alone that she can express, in her Valentine song, the most recessed and hidden of a young girl's fears and wishes, expresses powerfully the frailty of human existence, the irreparable losses it can sustain, the wreckage and flotsam that action, passion, and guilt leave in their wake. "Lord, we know what we are, but know not what we may be" is the leitmotif of the scenes, once more a study in concealments, but deeper and darker than that of the first act because what is concealed now on the stage, while it is revealed to the audience, is not a crime alone, but the sick soul of the Queen and the limed soul of the King, heavy with remorse of conscience. The songs and flowers of Ophelia are the mirrors in which each painfully and obliquely sees his own loss.

> Thought and affliction, passion, hell itself,
> She turns to favor and to prettiness,

Laertes says. Ophelia's shattered fragments, a madness unfeigned, unglossed, and unmitigated as no other in Shakespeare, and her death, represent the play's antithesis of human well-being, its maximum of human loss; and they provide the occasion for the graveyard scene, which articulates with an unmatched density of invention Hamlet's realization of absolute moral finitude.

The great traditional theme of *memento mori* is given a prologue before Hamlet's entrance in the fool's logic of the gravediggers, whose digging occupation is a reminder of the way of all fallen flesh since Adam. The Second Clown's worldy wisdom, "Will you ha' the truth on 't? If this had not been a gentlewoman, she should have been buried out o' Christian burial," reminds us of the specific fall—the turpitude in high places—that has been Hamlet's inheritance. The gravedigger's way with a syllogism is not Hamlet's, yet the issue of Hamlet's capability and godlike reason has scarcely proved happier, as the melancholy circumstances remind us. "Is she to be buried in Christian burial that wilfully seeks her own salvation?" "If I drown myself wittingly it argues an act. . . ." "Wilfully," "wittingly"—the words plunge in their trajectory to the heart of Hamlet's matter. That he will still, when he enters with Horatio, be unwitting of the grave's tenant to be is no small part of the irony. The mingling of comic and tragic modes in this encounter between prince and peasant is particularly effective because the perspective of common humanity which modifies and measures the spectator's response, and the protagonist's own extremity of desolation are here focused in one scene, and rendered by the gallows-wit duet between the gravedigger and his interlocutor. The protagonist himself, therefore, becomes the ironic vehicle for this most grimly comprehensive and ironic vision of the enigma and the paradox of existence.

The center of the scene is the familiar material of meditation in contempt of the world. But Hamlet's satirical *ubi sunt*—"Where be his quiddits now"—is transposed into quite another key by the revelation of the skull's identity. For a skull, most impersonal, most anonymous of all human relics, to have a name, and one which is bound up with Hamlet's childhood memories, brings into his reflections, with an inescapable, vivid immediacy, the whole impact of the vanished past—his own as well as the dark backward and abysm of time which is everyman's habitat. Death here is not eloquent, just, and mighty, but a stinking skull at which Hamlet's gorge rises. The base uses to which return the avatars of wit ("a fellow of infinite jest, of most excellent fancy") and of will ("that earth, which kept the world in awe") are obtrusively evident to him, agonizingly present to his senses and his imagination.

Nor does he seek the consolations of philosophy, of the grander verities. On the contrary, and despite Horatio's discouragement, he insists on tracing the noble dust of Alexander till he finds it stopping a bunghole. The poignance of his realization is thrown at once into relief and into perspective by the gravedigger's casual familiarity with the facts of his gruesome trade: "your water is a sore decayer of your whoreson dead body." Hamlet faces the facts of death, the deliquescent, the repulsive, the abhorrent outcome of a long day's dying that no paint can disguise for long. By comparison with this thanatopsis Hamlet's first invocation of death,

> O! that this too too solid flesh would melt,
> Thaw and resolve itself into a dew,

appears remote from reality: the yearning real enough, but the terms academic, as academic indeed as the attempt to resolve the riddles of passion and action — whether to suffer or to act, whether to live and endure or to make one's quietus with a bare bodkin — by ratiocination. Nor was it in direct contemplation of physical death that the "To be" soliloquy was spoken at all. Then death was conceived to be desirable, were it not for the dread of dreams — a sleep, a consummation devoutly to be wished, an end to griefs and burdens. That speech was the speech of a man who still struggled, despite his depression of spirit, against the admission of his own radical impotence to master his destiny; not of a man to whom the very idea of a destiny, his own or imperious Caesar's, is grotesque; not of a man mortified in the flesh by the knowledge of his nothingness.

But this stark humility is offset and modified by yet another shock, another revelation of an identity. Hamlet is precipitated out of his contemplation by the shock of the discovery that it is Ophelia who is to be buried with such "maimed rites." Her withdrawal from him in life is now to be sealed by the finality of the grave. And, still hidden, he hears himself traduced in Laertes' rhapsody of words, and is compelled to respond.

The double shock produces in him a revulsion of spirit, a new energy, an upsurge of passionate self-assertion. He leaps into the grave with a declaration of his royal identity. "This is I, Hamlet the Dane" announces that he dares, in the teeth of his adversary's ranting threats, to become who he is. The emotional sequence is almost exactly reproduced by Webster in *The Duchess of Malfi* in the second prison scene. The dramatization there is cruder, more explicit, as is the nature of the Duchess's ordeal; but "I am Duchess of Malfi still" registers no less movingly the reflex of proud defiance, the dignity of self-election. And his own rant to Laertes, in all its irascible spontaneity, reveals the deepest and most enduring preoccupations of the self he has striven throughout to realize. "What wilt thou do for her?" It is a theme upon which he will fight until his eyelids do no longer wag:

> 'Swounds, show me what thou'lt do;
> Woo't weep? woo't fight? woo't fast? woo't tear thyself?
> Woo't drink up eisel? eat a crocodile?
> I'll do't. Dost thou come here to whine?
> To outface me with leaping in her grave?
> Be buried quick with her, and so will I:
> And, if thou prate of mountains, let them throw
> Millions of acres on us, till our ground,
> Singeing his pate against the burning zone,
> Make Ossa like a wart! Nay, and thou'lt mouth,
> I'll rant as well as thou.
>
> (V.i.296–306)

Suffering, doing, saying. What action will suit the word, what word the action? What rhetoric but carries with it its own evasions and falsifications, becoming spurious in the very utterance?

Hamlet affirms at the end of the play "a divinity that shapes our ends, / Rough-hew them how we will," as the reality behind the shows and appearances of things. Of all Shakespeare's tragic heroes, he is the only one for whom a specifically Christian insight is the burden of his painfully acquired wisdom. Of the nominal Christians, Romeo is clearly in need of considerable religious instruction before he will qualify as Christian in any but a technical sense. Richard II's long dialogue with martyrdom ends with heroic, not saintly, self-assertion. Othello's Christianity is a *donnée* of the play, and of Othello's idea of himself; he repudiates it in a spasm of pagan savagery and he employs its imagery to articulate his sense of the enormity of his own most appalling deed; but its doctrines are never the subject of his cogitations, its truths never matter for reflection. For Macbeth the question is in abeyance, and this is one way in which the dreadful limbo in which he lives is defined. But for Hamlet Christian doctrine is an assumption and an ambience, the frame of his awareness, the implicit substance of his speculations, and the basis of his ethical sensibility. The observation that the code of revenge is anti-Christian is not to the purpose, for the Christian cultures accommodated, or at least failed to displace, the code of revenge for many centuries both before and after *Hamlet*.

It is to my mind a curiously perverse understanding that continues to claim, in the words of a distinguished recent commentator [H. Weisinger], that "Hamlet, though nominally a Christian, yet in moments of sharpest crises . . . turns to the consolations of Stoicism." He is speaking of Hamlet's defiance of augury: "If it be now, 'tis not to come; if it be not to come, it will be now; if it be not now, yet it will come; the readiness is all." True, it is a Senecan topos, but it is worth noticing that Hamlet is speaking in a moment not of sharp crisis but of calm decision; that he is, with a new kind of self-possession, calming the anxieties concerning premonitions of the stoical Horatio. This in itself makes its dramatic point. Moreover the evangelical affirmation that precedes the defiance of augury — "there's a special providence in the fall of a sparrow" — could hardly be more opposed to the Senecan-stoic view of the cosmos. These assertions in defiance of augury have a finality and a poise that is in marked contrast to the "interrogative mood" that has characterized Hamlet's idiom throughout:

> What's Hecuba to him or he to Hecuba,
> That he should weep for her?

> What is a man,
> If his chief good and market of his time
> Be but to sleep and feed

Did these bones cost no more the breeding, but to play at loggats with 'em?

Hamlet's realization of the folly of that self-assumption of wit whereby a man would be the artist of his own salvation, or another's, or another's damnation, has issued in fact in that most basic of mature Christian virtues: the patience, the self-control which waits upon the fullness of time in release both from anxiety and haste, passion and compulsion; which recognizes limitation with an objectivity that precludes panic.

The composure is dramatized to good effect in the encounter with Osric. Styles of response have been throughout the very stuff of Hamlet's judgments. He has expressed himself through his responses to them — his mother's, Claudius', the players', Horatio's, Polonius', Laertes'. What we know most deeply of Hamlet we know through his reactions to the styles of these others. Now the ridiculous Osric provides the occasion for a Hamlet in complete command of himself. Moreover, the parody of Osric's affectation serves to exhibit his self-possession, in marked contrast to the towering passion with which he responded to Laertes' bravery, in the court context in which we first became aware of its absence. The humor is of the kind that is the surest sign of stresses resolved in a play of intelligence. And it is shot through with sentences, such as "to know a man well, were to know himself" (V.ii.143–44), which strikes us as the very essence of a wisdom the entire sequence of events has distilled. Nevertheless, to find the final outcome of Hamlet's experience in this attainment of humility would be to do less than justice to the fine tragic balance of the catastrophe.

Hamlet kills his man, and one evil "canker of our nature" is destroyed in the full flush of its crimes. But not before it has destroyed him too, and his house, and seven other lives. What we are required to perceive at the close of the play, what the play strikes as its final note, is the enduring value of authentic individual existence; of the true record of what a man has made of himself and his circumstances. When Hamlet says "a man's life is no more than to say 'One,'" he also says "the interim is mine." And that the bearing of a wounded name should supremely matter is what we learn from Hamlet's plea to Horatio to absent him from felicity awhile, in order that the truth of the story should be made known. It is the final expression, at the very edge of silence, of a faith in the value of a life's integrity. Shakespeare has no tragedy which articulates an idea more magnanimous than this.

Tragic Alphabet

Lawrence Danson

"Speak to it. . . . It would be spoke to. . . . By heaven I charge thee, speak. . . . Speak to me. . . . O, Speak!" The word beats like a bell throughout the first scene of *Hamlet,* introducing (if obliquely) one of the play's central concerns even before we meet the prince. True, there are special difficulties involved in communicating with a ghost—the protocol is obscure at best, and it is understandable that the men on watch should be confused—but the problem of *speaking* extends far beyond that special case in the course of the play. Misunderstandings are among the most frequent phenomenon in *Hamlet:* Hamlet cannot or will not understand the language of the court, and the court, for its part, makes a desperate (and unsuccessful) attempt to understand the wild and whirling words of its prince. There is hardly a character with whom Hamlet does not become involved in a linguistic contretemps: Claudius and Gertrude have to remind him of (among other things) the proper kinship terms; Polonius, Rosencrantz, and Guildenstern—the interpreters Claudius sends to Hamlet—do not understand him; Ophelia does not understand his mad speeches and finally becomes, herself, "A document in madness"; while Osric and the Grave-digger (in their different ways) turn the tables on Hamlet and make *him* confess that "equivocation will undo us."

And the problem is not only verbal. The verbal difficulties mirror difficulties that exist in the realm of action—in the realm of what we might call gestural expression. Hamlet has a task to perform, a task real and deadly, but one also with a clearly symbolic dimension; his revenge must express a certain relationship to his

---

From *Tragic Alphabet: Shakespeare's Drama of Language.* © 1974 by Yale University. Yale University Press, 1974. Originally entitled "Hamlet."

dead father and to Claudius, to the state, to justice human and divine, and Hamlet finds that the acting of it becomes increasingly difficult as the incitements to it become more pressing. As it becomes difficult to say anything simply and directly in *Hamlet*, so it becomes difficult to do anything. And again the problem afflicts not only Hamlet but all who are involved with him: Claudius and those lesser beings "mortised and adjoined" to him are similarly driven to greater and greater indirections to find their directions out. The rottenness in Denmark has attacked the very roots of society — the symbolic systems which enable the primary social act, verbal and gestural expression.

The first instance of the problem suggests its dimensions and its cause. Marcellus and Bernardo have been unable to make the ghost speak; with a touching faith they have now called in a specialist: "Thou art a scholar; speak to it, Horatio" (I.i.42). But even Horatio is ill-equipped to break through the impasse in communication. He barrages the voiceless ghost with exhortation and finally, in frustration, calls for force; they strike at it with their partisans only to realize, "We do it wrong, being so majestical, / To offer it the show of violence" (I.i.143). Horatio, Bernardo, and Marcellus are, of course, the wrong men to deal with the ghost:

> Let us impart what we have seen to-night
> Unto young Hamlet; for, upon my life,
> This spirit, dumb to us, will speak to him.
>
> (I.i.169)

But they lack more than the proper relationship. They lack the language (words) and the other means (gestures, and words and gestures ordered as ritual) that would make communication possible. They are ignorant of protocol, confused about the sort of ceremony to use — here in the night, on the battlements, amidst the "posthaste and romage" of wartime — when addressing "the king / That was and is the question of these wars." The ghost, that is to say, is a wholly new element, undreamed of in their philosophy; it is an anomaly, and there is no customary language, no ritual, for dealing with it.

Even *before* we see the ghost we may find indications that the problem in Denmark involves the failure of ritual. The very first words of the play are an inversion of ceremonial order:

BERNARDO. Who's there?
FRANCISCO. Nay, answer me. Stand and unfold yourself.

And the men on guard, it appears, do not even know what it is they are guarding against — only that it is something extraordinary. "Good now, sit down, and tell me, he that knows," Marcellus asks,

Why this same strict and most observant watch
So nightly toils the subject of the land;
And why such daily cast of brazen cannon,
And foreign mart for implements of war;
Why such impress of shipwrights, whose sore task
Does not divide the Sunday from the week;
What might be toward, that this sweaty haste
Doth make the night joint-labourer with the day:
Who is't that can inform me?

(I.i.70)

The dissolving of difference between Sunday and the rest of the week, and between night and day, are small touches, but they are of a piece with the other "strange eruptions" — of which the ghost is the strangest — that have deprived the men of the certainties of custom and ceremonial. In scene IV, when Hamlet joins the watch, the men question him, not only about the ghost, but about the customs of King Claudius as well. Despite "kettledrum and trumpet," even Claudius fails to make himself understood; even the rituals of the king fail to communicate their meanings.

In this context it is worth noting that the ghost, in speaking to Hamlet, dwells especially on the rituals that were denied him; he was

Cut off even in the blossoms of my sin,
Unhous'led, disappointed, unanel'd;
No reck'ning made, but sent to my account
With all my imperfections on my head.

(I.v.76)

The murder was "most foul, strange, and unnatural" — and it receives this triple emphasis presumably because of the many social bonds it canceled: it was both fratricide and political assassination, and it followed acts of adultery and incest. Now the ghost must "walk the night" until "the foul crimes . . . Are burnt and purg'd away" (I.v.12).

The murder of old Hamlet is the first of the "maimed rites" in the play; others follow, especially in matters of death and interment. Polonius and Ophelia both receive "hugger-mugger" burials, and the series ends only with the play's bloody final scene. Laertes, with his bold complaints to Claudius about his father's

means of death, his obscure funeral —
No trophy, sword, nor hatchment, o'er his bones,
No noble rite nor formal ostentation —

(IV.v.209)

and his rant (as Hamlet calls it) over Ophelia's curtailed funeral, is most blatant in expressing his displeasure at the absence of the old expressive modes. But Hamlet, whose vision is deeper and whose denunciation is more subtle, sees what Laertes cannot, that the old terms of "honor" — the old rituals and (as we shall see) language itself — have become rotten and will no longer serve. The murder of old Hamlet and his reappearance in ghostly form introduce a fatal anomaly that destroys ritual observance and makes the demand for a new ritual that can accommodate it. The injunction to Hamlet to revenge includes the implicit demand for a new, expressive language.

When we turn from the battlements to the court we find the anomaly embodied in Hamlet himself. Amidst the celebrants of a marriage and a coronation, the prince sits silently apart, mourning a death and a usurpation. For Claudius this stark anomaly is intolerable, and his language reflects his method of dealing with it. The oxymorons of his opening speech are a desperate gambit, an attempt to make language swallow up irreconcilable differences:

> Therefore our sometime sister, now our queen . . .
> Have we, as 'twere with a defeated joy,
> With an auspicious and a dropping eye,
> With mirth in funeral, and with dirge in marriage,
> In equal scale weighing delight and dole,
> Taken to wife.
>
> (I.ii.8, 10)

But this weighing is a mere trick: the words alone balance and cancel each other out. Still, the trick might work; the courtiers, after all, have in their "better wisdoms . . . freely gone with this affair along." Only Hamlet is there to remind them of a reality not so easily manipulated.

If Claudius's mode is the oxymoron, Hamlet's is the pun. One man balances words to cancel out their antithetical meanings, while the other overbalances words *with* meanings. The pun thus typifies Hamlet's role throughout the play: it is the linguistic confrontation that precedes the physical. Claudius greets Hamlet as "my cousin Hamlet, and my son," but Hamlet responds (aside), "A little more than kin, and less than kind" (I.ii.64, 65) — informing us that Claudius's double kinship is (through the pun on "kind") both unnatural and ungracious, not at all of Hamlet's kind. "How is it that the clouds still hang on you," asks Claudius; and in Hamlet's reply — "Not so my lord; I am too much in the sun" (66, 67) — the sunshine of royal attention and the too-much sonship of double paternity become a distaste for life itself (the condition of being in the sun). "Thou know'st 'tis common — all that lives must die," says Gertrude (showing a touch of the Claudian manner in her facile balancing of *lives* with *die*):

"Aye, madam, it is common," comes Hamlet's reply (72, 74), but now the word *common* is loaded with meanings that quite reverse the ameliorating effects of the oxymoron. Hamlet's punning carries with it the demand that words receive their full freight of meaning, and it is a demand that dooms to defeat Claudius's wordy attempts at compromise.

An "exchange of complementary values" is the essential act of social existence. At the linguistic level, "there must be a certain equivalence between the symbols used by the addresser and those known and interpreted by the addressee" [Roman Jakobson and Morris Halle, *Fundamentals of Language*] to assure the success of any speech event. But at the opening of *Hamlet* (as the exchanges between Hamlet and Claudius and Gertrude show), the absence of "complementary values," of equivalent symbols, is indeed remarkable. The one word *common* conveys ideas so widely different to two speakers as to suggest that it is really two separate words. And there is no equivalence in the use of such vital symbols as *mother, father, uncle, nephew,* and *son.* Claudius's oxymoronic mode is an attempt to enforce the illusion that the symbols are univocal, while Hamlet's puns expose the equivocation that has invaded each.

So it is, too, in the other, gestural language of social transactions. "My lord, I came to see your father's funeral" (I.ii.176), Horatio tells Hamlet, but even a "funeral" is now an ambiguous symbol: "I prithee do not mock me, fellow student; I think it was to see my mother's wedding." In the midst of the celebrating court, Hamlet's very dress and demeanor—his "nighted colour" and "vailed lids" —are a sort of silent pun, loading the values of "funeral" onto those of "marriage." Later in the play, when we see Hamlet baiting Polonius—

> What do you read, my lord?
> HAMLET. Words, words, words.
> POLONIUS. What is the matter, my lord?
> HAMLET. Between who?
> POLONIUS. I mean, the matter that you read, my lord—
> (II.ii.190)

we will be seeing nothing different in kind from what our first glimpse of Hamlet has already revealed. Hamlet cannot, or will not, understand the language of the court—a language which (as Hamlet shows Polonius in the matter of the shape-shifting cloud) has lost its necessary relationship to a world it no longer adequately describes.

Hamlet's puns continually probe a structural flaw in the edifice of Denmark, threatening to bring the building down on all their heads. He consistently brings together the balanced opposites of the Claudian oxymoron and pressurizes the contradiction to the breaking point. Closely related to his technique of aggressive punning is the use he makes of the syllogism. It is not sufficient that the king and queen should be (as in his parody of the Claudian manner he calls them) "my uncle-father and aunt-mother" (II.ii.372); by syllogistic reasoning Hamlet arrives at the reductio ad absurdam where the king is simply "dear mother" — since "father and mother is man and wife; man and wife is one flesh; and so, my mother" (IV.iii.49).

As a Wittenberg man, Hamlet knows the central importance of the syllogism as a tool of traditional (that is, scholastic) philosophy. But here, in using the syllogism to expose a false, absurd situation, he sounds more like the skeptical Francis than like the scholastic Friar Bacon. In his critique of the "idols of the market-place," Francis Bacon was to denounce the errors which arise when the language we use fails to correspond to the truth of things-behind-language. And the syllogism would be a special point of Bacon's attack; as his case has been put by a modern historian [Frederick Copleston]:

> The syllogism consists of propositions; and propositions consist of words; and words express concepts. Thus, if the concepts are confused and if they are the result of over-hasty abstractions, nothing which is built on them is secure.

What Hamlet shows by his use of the syllogism is that nothing secure can rest on the falsehood that masquerades as the royal order of Denmark.

From Claudius's point of view, however, the syllogism is simply mad: its logic is part of Hamlet's "antic disposition." Sane men know, after all, that "man and wife is one flesh" only in a metaphoric or symbolic sense; they know that only a madman would look for literal truth in linguistic conventions. And Claudius is right that such "madness in great ones must not unwatched go" (III.i.end). For the madman, precisely because he does not accept society's compromises and because he explores its conventions for meanings they cannot bear, exposes the flaws which "normal" society keeps hidden. Hamlet's wordplay, "pregnant" as it is with matters normally left undisclosed, brings to light things which (as Polonius says) "reason and sanity could not so prosperously be delivered of" (II.ii.208). Hamlet's very language — a language that is a continual probing of language — brings the conventions and the compromises inexorably to view.

And not only Hamlet's: the threat that madness, and mad-speech, poses to the state is shown in Ophelia too. (For, as I have already said, Hamlet's problem becomes the problem of all who are associated with him. The distance between reality and the language that ostensibly describes it in Denmark, that builds equivocation into that language and leaves Hamlet speaking his antic wordplay, leaves Ophelia, too, speaking madly.) The disorder of Ophelia's speech — its departure from the intelligible norm — is even more significant, and threatening, than its actual content. A gentleman says of her:

> She speaks much of her father; says she hears
> There's tricks i' th' world, and hems, and beats her heart;
> Spurns enviously at straws; speaks things in doubt,
> That carry but half sense. Her speech is nothing.
> Yet the unshaped use of it doth move
> The hearers to collection; they yawn at it,
> And botch the words up fit to their own thoughts;
> Which, as her winks and nods and gestures yield them,
> Indeed would make one think there might be thought,
> Though nothing sure, yet much unhappily.
>
> (IV.v.4)

Here is the genius of great grief: Ophelia, no longer able to contain or express her experience within the bounds of "normal" behavior, finds in the virtual silence of madness the most effective, and for Claudius the most damning, speech of all. Any charges against Claudius, rationally delivered, could be rationally answered — as Claudius does indeed answer Laertes. But the charge that comes from the realm of madness is too sweeping; its very mode implies that the ordinary language is itself being condemned, and will not serve in reply.

Now no one has ever suggested (as far as I know) that Ophelia is only shamming; she has no choice about the way she speaks. But Hamlet is another matter and, even without solving the red herring of his real versus his feigned madness, we must agree that Hamlet's choice of language needs some further explanation. Most of the rest of the court sees nothing wrong with the ordinary expressive modes; Gertrude, for instance, sees nothing wrong with her use of the word *common*. Why then does Hamlet, even before the ghost appears to him, reject the language of the court, and with it the compromises that would assure a smooth social functioning? Why must the expression he seeks (which, after the ghost's appearance, will become identified with his revenge) be found outside the conventional modes available?

Lucien Goldmann defines "two essential characteristics of tragic man" which may be applied as well to our Shakespearean hero as to the Racinian heroes he discusses:

> the first is that he makes [an] exclusive and absolute demand for impossible values; and the second is that, as a result of this, his demand is for "all or nothing," and he is totally indifferent to degrees and approximations, and to any concept containing the idea of relativity.

The self-negating oxymorons of Claudian rhetoric, disguising actual conflict under a show of verbal concord, reflect the sort of condition this absolutist man must find intolerable. Hamlet's disgust with the equivocal language—both words and rituals—of the Danish court leads him to his "all or nothing" attitude toward all language and ritual.

Equivocation—the conflict between the reality Hamlet perceives and the language used to describe that reality—has made all expression a matter of mere seeming, and Hamlet knows not seems. His rejection of the Claudian language extends to a rejection of all the symbolic systems that can denote a man. Thus, even his own punning (both verbal and silent) is inadequate: Hamlet chooses "nothing" since he cannot have "all":

> 'Tis not alone my inky cloak, good mother,
> Nor customary suits of silent black,
> Nor windy suspiration of forc'd breath,
> No, nor the fruitful river in the eye,
> Nor the dejected haviour in the visage,
> Together with all forms, moods, shapes of grief,
> That can denote me truly. These, indeed, seem;
> For they are actions that a man might play;
> But I have that within which passes show—
> These but the trappings and the suits of woe.
>
> (I.ii.77)

In an ambiguous world, where all is but seeming, and hence misinterpretation, no symbol is successful. The absolutist Hamlet finds nothing that can denote him truly, and is driven back to the only place where indubitable truth can reside, to the self: "But I have that within which passes show."

Hamlet's insistence upon an inner essence of truth is both noble and peculiarly jejune; it is the youthful nobility which refuses to compromise between the self and the world. For such a man, the self has a value independent of its suits and trappings, and he demands that it be prized and satisfied without regard to that accidental matter, the body, which happens to go with it. There is a poem by John Donne which wittily exposes the inevitable defeat of such youthful idealism. In "The Blossome," Donne takes quite literally the duality of mind and body; and, as he is about to leave for a libertine visit to London, he addresses the heart which would stay behind in faithfulness to a denying mistress:

> Well then, stay here; but know,
> When thou hast stayd and done thy most;
> A naked thinking heart, that makes no show,
> Is to a woman, but a kinde of Ghost;

> How shall shee know my heart; or having none,
> Know thee for one?
> Practice may make her know some other part,
> But take my word, shee doth not know a Heart.

"A naked thinking heart, that makes no show" (or: "that within which passes show"): it cannot be; it is a mere immanence (a "Ghost") needing a bodying forth in expressive action. As Hamlet tries to come to terms with the need for body and action, he shows a bitterness not unlike Donne's ("Practice may make her know some other part"); for a while in Hamlet's play, the only expressive action that seems possible is "lust in action." Hamlet's frequent expressions of sexual digust project, in part, his feeling that the soul is raped in its commerce with the world. To speak or act in a world where all speech and action are equivocal seeming is, for Hamlet, both perilous and demeaning, a kind of whoring.

The whole vexed question of Hamlet's delay ought, I believe, to be considered in light of this dilemma. To a man alienated from his society's most basic symbolic modes, who finds all speech and action mere seeming and hypocritical playing, comes an imperious demand to speak and act — to express himself in deed his father's son. The ghost's stress upon ritual modes indicates that the expression demanded must not be just "a kind of wild justice," but an expression ordered and meaningful. Hamlet's difficulties at the linguistic level — his puns and "antic disposition," the lack of commensurate values between him and the rest of the court — are reflected in his difficulties at the level of action. Like Titus Andronicus, Hamlet is confronted with the expressive imperative; and the demanded expression, the act of revenge, must be an unequivocal gesture in a world where all gesture has become equivocal seeming. Hamlet must satisfy not only his dead father's needs, but also his own deepest need to be denoted truly.

The problems of expression which confront Hamlet, as I have so far discussed them, are peculiar to his world — to the Denmark constituted in murder, usurpation, incest, and adultery. But there is a further problem revealed in the course of the play, related to these but central, not only for Hamlet, but for tragic man generally. It is most fully enunciated, appropriately enough, by that tragedian of the city, the Player-King. It is the problem of time, or history, and of expression-in-time. Briefly, how can one speak or act (truly) in a world where each succeeding moment gives the last the lie, where our words are no sooner uttered than they are relegated to a discredited past and (like Achilles racing the inexorable tortoise) can never overtake the truth of the passing moment? In "The Murder of Gonzago," the Player-Queen protests that she will never remarry after her husband's death; to which he replies, in lines worth quoting extensively:

> I do believe you think what now you speak;
> But what we do determine oft we break.

> Purpose is but the slave to memory,
> Of violent birth, but poor validity;
> Which now, the fruit unripe, sticks on the tree;
> But fall unshaken when they mellow be.
> Most necessary 'tis that we forget
> To pay ourselves what to ourselves is debt.
> What to ourselves in passion we propose,
> The passion ending, doth the purpose lose.
> The violence of either grief or joy
> Their own enactures with themselves destroy.
> Where joy most revels grief doth most lament;
> Grief joys, joy grieves, on slender accident.
> This world is not for aye; nor 'tis not strange
> That even our loves should with our fortunes change.
>
> But, orderly to end where I begun,
> Our wills and fates do so contrary run
> That our devices still are overthrown;
> Our thoughts are ours, their ends none of our own.
>   (III.ii.181, 205)

The Player-King does not question his wife's sincerity: the irrelevance of sincerity is part of the problem. He questions, rather, the validity of any assertion of purpose made in a world where (to quote a more pithy tragic figure) thoughts are the slaves of life and life is time's fool. Even where thought and expression are in tune with each other, the inevitable movement of time ("fate") makes a liar of our "wills." In this world of constant process, "Our thoughts are ours, their ends none of our own."

Inexorably moving time is the discreditor of all purpose and action: it is the primary equivocator, and for the man who despises all seeming it raises hypocrisy to the level of a universal condition. Claudius, who knows and accepts the conditions of this world as fully as Hamlet knows and rejects them, is in accord with the Player-King on this point. Claudius has been trying to win over Laertes; and he knows that Laertes (whose expressions of love for Polonius and determination to be revenged are made with "emphasis" enough) still may be, as Claudius puts it, "Like the painting of a sorrow, / A face without a heart" (IV.vii.108). For Laertes's determination, like that of the Player-Queen, is the slave of time: "I know," Claudius says, that

> love is begun by time,
> And that I see, in passages of proof,

> Time qualifies the spark and fire of it.
> There lives within the very flame of love
> A kind of wick or snuff that will abate it;
> And nothing is at a like goodness still;
> For goodness, growing to a pleurisy,
> Dies in his own too much.
>
> (IV.vii.111)

Claudius, like the Player-King, does not doubt the intention: he is simply stating a general law, and it is the very absoluteness which makes it so terrible. His crafty answer to the problem of action-in-time is really no answer at all, but mere accommodation; it is simply a *carpe diem* which avoids the problem:

> That we would do,
> We should do when we would; for this "would" changes,
> And hath abatements and delays as many
> As there are tongues, are hands, are accidents. . . .
>
> (IV.vii.118)

Laertes can show himself indeed his father's son by getting rid of Hamlet the nearest way. And Claudius's incitement to immediate action sounds as though it might do as a prescription for Hamlet as well, whose own task is mirrored by Laertes's. Claudius's advice would make either man an effective killer—but it would still leave them (what Hamlet refuses to be) the fools of time.

The problem of time's discrediting effects upon human actions and intentions is what makes Hamlet's "To be, or not to be" soliloquy eternal dilemma rather than fulfilled dialectic. Faced with the uncertainty of any action, an uncertainty that extends even to the afterlife, Hamlet, too, finds the "wick or snuff" of which Claudius speaks: "Thus conscience"—by which Hamlet means, I take it, not only scruples but all thoughts concerning the future—

> does make cowards of us all;
> And thus the native hue of resolution
> Is sicklied o'er with the pale cast of thought,
> And enterprises of great pitch and moment,
> With this regard, their currents turn awry
> And lose the name of action.—
>
> (III.i.83)

Both the Player-King and Claudius discuss the temporal dilemma in regard to love; here, Hamlet's reflections are broken off as he catches sight of Ophelia. In the final act, Hamlet will declare, "I loved Ophelia," but at the midway point of his play the distressing thought that what-we-are-now is not what-we-will-become makes love seem only one more hypocrisy in a world of hypocrisy:

> OPHELIA. My lord, I have remembrances of yours
> That I have longed long to re-deliver.
> I pray you now receive them.
> HAMLET. No, not I;
> I never gave you ought.
>
> (III.i.83)

For the gestures of yesterday are false today.

> HAMLET. I did love you once.
> OPHELIA. Indeed, my lord, you made me believe so.
> HAMLET. You should not have believ'd me; for virtue
> cannot so inoculate our old stock but we shall relish
> of it. I loved you not.
> OPHELIA. I was the more deceived.
>
> (III.i.115)

The only way out of the dilemma of action falsified in the acting is to remove oneself somehow from the mortal condition: "Get thee to a nunnery. Why wouldst thou be a breeder of sinners?"

Ophelia is not only Hamlet's victim; in her limited way, she faces the same difficulties which cause him to victimize her. She, too, lives in a world of hypocritical seeming, erected (in her case) into the self-serving morality of Polonius's and Laertes's admonitions. Laertes warns her not to trust Hamlet's expressions of love, and one of the reasons he gives is that same simple reason Hamlet (with self-mocking bitterness) also gives — man is subject to time:

> For nature crescent does not grow alone
> In thews and bulk, but as this temple waxes,
> The inward service of the mind and soul
> Grows wide withal. Perhaps he loves you now.
>
> (I.iii.11)

Polonius adds the limbs and outward flourishes to Laertes's lesson, in words recalled later by Claudius's speech:

> These blazes, daughter,
> Giving more light than heat — extinct in both,
> Even in their promise, as it is a-making —
> You must not take for fire.
>
> (I.iii.117)

(Claudius says, "There lives within the very flame of love / A kind of wick or snuff.") Even as it is spoken, according to Polonius, the word becomes false. And

Hamlet, for the greater part of his play, would have to give his bitter assent: only silence (and inaction) can be true to that which is within.

The Polonii are concerned in a practical manner with the problem of time and growth, that man changes and therefore will be false. Hamlet takes the question the necessary one step further; man *dies,* and his death is the ultimate change that makes liars of us all. The graveyard, with Yorick's skull, is to Hamlet a most powerful symbol; it is, at least for a time, his proof that all action contains a principle of obsolescence. Alexander's world-conquering gestures are rendered as meaningless by the grave as Yorick's gibes and gambols. Death proves that all our words and deeds are as transient, and thus ultimately false, as a lady's cosmetics: "Now get you to my lady's chamber, and tell her, let her paint an inch thick, to this favour she must come" (V.i.189). Horatio's comment, "'Twere to consider too curiously to consider so," is a counsel of simple sanity, for Hamlet's consideration would make all "enterprises . . . their currents turn awry / And lose the name of action." But Hamlet, who has seen and considered too much to turn away now, will have to achieve his expressive action, not with eyes averted from the skull, but with the fact of death integrated in the gesture he will make.

The arrival of the players in Act II, scene ii gathers to a focus many of the apparently disparate thematic concerns of *Hamlet;* most immediately, the coming of the players bears upon the problem of expression in a world of seeming. For these players, unlike others at Elsinore, confess their profession proudly; they are very much experts in seeming, bringing with them the gossip of the green room and merging into one complex image Hamlet's Denmark and Shakespeare's Globe Theater. Because they are actors, they have a concern for rhetoric and gesture: their very presence thus serves to remind us of the difficulty men have had at Elsinore in finding a language with which to speak to the ghost and to each other. We have been watching a king (Claudius) play his very difficult role, and have seen the difficulty of that role vastly increased by the prince's rejection of all seeming and playing. Now the prince exclaims, "He that plays the king shall be welcome" (II.ii.317)

The scene in which the players make their entrance has already acquainted us with a variety of uses for playing. Polonius has proposed a solution to the problem of Hamlet's madness, and in the process has been cautioned to speak "more matter with less art" (II.ii.95). "Madam, I swear I use no art at all," the artful Polonius responds, and then proposes, as a means for getting at the truth, an improvisation with himself and Claudius as hidden audience, and with his daughter as ingénue to Hamlet's unsuspecting romantic lead. Hamlet then treats Polonius to a private show of his feigned madness—a difficult play full of allusions and puns which seems to Polonius "pregnant" with a meaning "which reason and sanity could not so prosperously be delivered of." Polonius fails to recognize the madness as acting, but he does see a "method" in it. Finally, Rosencrantz and Guildenstern, playing the parts given them by Claudius, also use seeming to find out a truth and are met in turn with a seeming (Hamlet's) which may well be truth.

The arrival of the players at this point breaks through the tangle of involved wordplay, apparent irrelevance, and politic dissembling. Hamlet's greeting to them is warm, with a controlled excitement which seems to come from what Bradley calls "the true Hamlet, the Hamlet of the days before his father's death." [Perhaps Hamlet already sees in them a form of release from his noncommunicative tangle: his greeting rushes directly on to a hope:] "We'll have a speech straight. Come, give us a taste of your quality; come, a passionate speech" (II.ii.425).

Robert J. Nelson, writing of the convention in general, has said that, "The play within a play is the theater reflecting on itself, on its own paradoxical seeming." The Player's speech about Pyrrhus, Priam, and Hecuba is, as it were, merely a curtain raiser to the more elaborate "The Murder of Gonzago" in Act III; but it is a true play-within-a-play in providing, to paraphrase Professor Nelson, a reflection of the play *Hamlet's* paradoxical seeming, and it is worth pausing over. Polonius finds it too long, but Hamlet is both moved and perplexed by it — by the speech itself and by the circumstances of its delivery. The Player's speech, as we shall see, brings to consciousness for Hamlet the nexus of ideas: playing-sincerity-expression-revenge.

One "reflection" is succinctly recognized in Harry Levin's analysis of the Player's speech:

> To the observer who is painfully learning the distinction between *seems* and *is*, the hideous pangs of the Trojan Queen are the mirrored distortions of Gertrude's regal insincerities. The "damn'd defeat" of Priam, reminding Hamlet of his father, prompts him to renounce his hitherto passive role, to soliloquize on the Player's example, and finally to evolve his plan of action.

What Hamlet sees, that is to say, is in part the murder of a father — a murder recounted in a high heroical vein which is, in itself, a painful reminder of his own lack of heroism. But the mirror a play holds up to nature — which in the case of a play-*within*-a-play means the "nature" of the containing play — has curious properties, not the least of which is its ability to reflect more than one scene or set of images simultaneously.

Thus we need not be unduly surprised by a second "reflection" found in the Player's speech — a reflection which shows Hamlet's form in that of the father-murderer Pyrrhus. Here is the picture of Pyrrhus at the instant when he hears the "hideous crash" of "senseless Ilium" falling as if in sympathy with Priam:

> For, lo! his sword,
> Which was declining on the milky head
> Of reverend Priam, seem'd i' th' air to stick.
> So, as a painted tyrant, Pyrrhus stood
> And, like a neutral to his will and matter,
> Did nothing.
> But, as we often see, against some storm,
> A silence in the heavens, the rack stand still,
> The bold winds speechless, and the orb below
> As hush as death, anon the dreadful thunder
> Doth rend the region; so, after Pyrrhus' pause,
> A roused vengeance sets him new a-work;
> And never did the Cyclops' hammer fall
> On Mars's armour, forg'd for proof eterne,
> With less remorse than Pyrrhus' bleeding sword
> Now falls on Priam.
>
> (II.ii.471)

Hamlet, "like a neutral to his will and matter," has been hesitating in the acting of *his* revenge (for Pyrrhus, too, is a revenger); and Hamlet, too, has heard the "hideous crash" of a society's central edifice and symbol. The enacting of his revenge has come to seem like the cataclysm of an entire world.

The momentary identification between Hamlet and Pyrrhus does not yet exhaust the image. Plays-within-a-play tend, I have suggested, to reflect the nature of dramatic art itself; they present an image, not only of this play's thematic concerns, but of this play as any or all plays. And thus the image of Pyrrhus as "painted tyrant"—an image associated, by the epithet, with forms of art—expresses something of the nature of the tragic drama. It is an image of energy in stasis, of an eternally suspended moment—suspended first because it is called "painted," and also because of the retarding motion of the verse here, with its long, swelling epic simile—an eternal moment preceding the inexorable fall of the tragic blow.

This static instant—which, while only an instant, is also an eternity fixed by poet and painter—is a demonstration of the esthetic fact that, in the Player's play, Troy will always fall, that Hecuba will always lament, and that the audience will always sympathize—and thus that Troy will never fall utterly. The permanence of the image, and of its potential effect upon an audience, is important in understanding Hamlet's reaction to it. Imaged in the pregnant instant of "Pyrrhus' pause" is the optimistic distinction between life and art expressed for our modern world by Pirandello:

> All that lives, by the fact of living, has a form, and by the same token
> must die—except the work of art which lives forever in so far as it *is*
> form.

In the world of flux and mere appearance which baffles Hamlet's search for an adequate expression, a play—apparently the most insubstantial of phenomena—moves Hamlet deeply. He wanted "a passionate speech," and that he surely got. Nor can we dismiss the Player's speech as mere literary travesty: whatever objections we might make to it—its strange words, overelaboration, emotional excess—are the same objections made by the audience at Elsinore, as if Shakespeare specifically wanted to forestall and disarm our criticism. Indeed the speech does (in Dryden's phrase) "smell too strongly of the buskin"; but, Harry Levin recognizes, this is an integral part of the *trompe l'oeil* effect by which the play-within-the-play makes the equally conventional primary play (that it, *Hamlet* itself) stand out as primary reality. The self-consciously "poetic" style of the Player's speech forces us to recognize it as something apart from Hamlet's accustomed world. Like Hamlet, savoring and questioning that word *mobled,* we are forced to attend to the language of the Player's speech: because it calls attention to itself as poetry, its language is "corporealized" [Burkhardt]; it pulls us up short as we confront those devices—its alliterations, invocations, epic similes, archaisms, and so on—which tell us that this is not the "transparent" language of ordinary discourse. We need not like the language of the Player's speech, though I think we ought, but we cannot dismiss it. Hamlet, at least, does not.

Hamlet responds eagerly to this professional in the arts of expression. Indeed, he gives the Player the sincerest flattery: his imitation of the Player's speech follows after Polonius has been bid to "see the players well bestowed" and the stage is again clear. The similarity between Hamlet's soliloquy ("O, what a rouge and peasant slave am I!") and the Player's speech was noticed by Dover Wilson, who writes that "The two speeches are for all the world like a theme given out by the First Violin and then repeated by the soloist." Repeated, however, with important variations. But the musical analogy is apt because the similarity between the player's speech and Hamlet's soliloquy is very much one of tone and rhythm.

Hamlet's speech, like the Player's, builds to a crescendo of sound and emotion:

> Am I a coward?
> Who calls me villain, breaks my pate across,
> Plucks off my beard and blows it in my face,
> Tweaks me by the nose, gives me the lie i' th' throat
> As deep as to the lungs? Who does me this?
> Ha!

> 'Swounds, I should take it; for it cannot be
> But I am pigeon-liver'd and lack gall
> To make oppression bitter, or ere this
> I should'a fatted all the region kites
> With this slave's offal. Bloody, bawdy villain!
> Remorseless, treacherous, lecherous, kindless villain!
> O, vengeance!
>
> > (II.ii.565)

And here Hamlet's speech, like the Player's at the instant when Pyrrhus's ear is taken prisoner, stops suddenly in its hurtling career. Hamlet, too, is caught in an attitude of listening, suspended while his own roaring declamation dies away. Then:

> Why, what an ass am I! This is most brave,
> That I, the son of a dear father murder'd,
> Prompted to my revenge by heaven and hell,
> Must, like a whore, unpack my heart with words,
> And fall a-cursing like a very drab,
> A scullion!
>
> > (II.ii.578)

The moment of stasis ended, Hamlet's speech moves rapidly, surely, with a new sense of purpose, to the announcement of a plan of action. The conclusion comes as swiftly and irrevocably as Pyrrhus's deadly blow; and the speech which begins as a reflection on the nature of acting ends with the announcement of the tragic peripety: "The play's the thing / Wherein I'll catch the conscience of the King."

Something curious has happened between the two speeches: the variation on the theme. For the Player's speech, a speech that is decisively "play" and makes no illusory claims to be "real," is wholly successful in its expression; but, the "play" now over, the words of passion become in Hamlet's mouth a mere unpacking, a whorishness. And this, as Hamlet recognizes, is most strange. A player has moved himself and his audience to tears on behalf of a mere fiction; Hamlet now, at his most sincere and most truly impassioned, finds that his sincerity falls far short of a player's seeming, that his true passion is more theatrical and less satisfying than a player's part.

The question Hamlet puts initially stands halting between the existential and the purely esthetic:

> What's Hecuba to him or he to Hecuba,
> That he should weep for her? What would he do,

> Had he the motive and the cue for passion
> That I have?

(II.ii.552)

And the quick answer he gives is as psychologically useless as it is esthetically naïve: "He would drown the stage with tears, / And cleave the general ear with horrid speech." Hamlet tries to do precisely this, as we have seen, going faster and faster, louder and louder, working himself up only to stop short and condemn himself for cursing "like a drab." What goes wrong? Why doesn't the Player's way work for Hamlet?

Since a part of Hamlet's perplexity has to do with the choice of words and their mode of delivery, a part of our answer must also deal with the linguistic medium. And so we may notice that the Player's old-fashioned declamation was alive in the timelessness of its play: it stood out from the general buzz and hum of Denmark's language and earned for itself the right to be attended to fully. But Hamlet is imprisoned in history, a fool of time, and his words are the realm's current coin. Hamlet's words are as good as such words can be, but (as he will later tell Laertes) anyone can "mouth" and "rant" them; and despite all the emphasis in the world, the loudest word in a worn-out language might as well be a whisper. At this stage of the action, we might say, Hamlet's play (unlike the Player's play of Pyrrhus and Priam) is not yet written: because he lives he is tied to a form, but it is the form of the dying animal; it is a form that lives in history, and so gives itself the lie at every successive moment of its being. Hamlet's passion becomes false in the very speaking of it, and this (we recall) is precisely the thing he feared when we first saw him, alone and silent, nursing that inner core of unexpressed truth which alone was trustworthy.

But there is more. For the expression Hamlet seeks is one that words alone could never accomplish. Hamlet demands an expression in action, and so we may notice that it is action which the Player's speech contains but Hamlet's lacks. Poet and painter have embodied the form of Pyrrhus's revenge, and when the Player speaks his lines, the words give renewed life to this action which has been made eternal form. But Hamlet has before him still the task of uniting the proper action with his words, of informing his words with meaning through gesture. Before the meeting with his father's ghost, Hamlet thought he must be content with what was within. Now the players have come and shown him the potential of "acting"; but immediately he has found the difficulty and double-edgedness of it. Not just any acting will do, and not all words. Still, somehow, "The play's the thing."

I am trying to find an answer to the question, "What does Hamlet find in the players' art?" and I am aware that the answer I am proposing is a tortuous

one. I am aware, too, that there is an easier answer: we could simply say that
Hamlet recalls a commonplace about the affective powers of drama —

> That guilty creatures, sitting at a play,
> Have by the very cunning of the scene
> Been struck so to the soul that presently
> They have proclaim'd their malefactions —
>
> (II.ii.585)

and decides to use the theater as a sort of lie-detector test. Is it, then, only a
modern consciousness, seeing *Hamlet* through the redactions of Pirandello or
Tom Stoppard, which will want to find more here than the obvious lesson in
criminology?

The fact is that *Hamlet,* through any eyes, is insistently self-conscious about
its own histrionic basis. And in a theater like Shakespeare's, where the metaphor
of life-as-drama was never far away, could the situation of Hamlet's soliloquy be
dismissed? — a player in a play (the actor playing Hamlet in *Hamlet*) gives a speech
about a player playing a player within his play, and in that speech considers the
relationships between appearance and reality, histrionics and sincerity, acting and
action. A degree of subtlety seems warranted.

And there are other indications that the answer to Hamlet's questions about
the players' art, his troubled

> What would he do,
> Had he the motive and the cue for passion
> That I have?

involves more than simply proving Claudius's guilt. For the lie-detector use of
acting is one we see much of in *Hamlet,* and though it shares certain characteristics with Hamlet's use of acting, it is decisively not the same. Polonius is the
great master of it — of using, that is, the indirection or downright falseness of acting to discover a truth. Polonius was in his time an amateur actor himself; appropriately, he played Caesar and was killed in the capitol. But we now see Polonius
either as a theater critic (and it is a flat sort of criticism he practices, multiplying
rigid categories while demanding that he be kept entertained), or as a director — of Laertes, Reynaldo, Ophelia, Gertrude. To each he recommends the use
of seeming: in the case of Laertes it is to be nothing short of a life-style, but with
the others it is specifically a means for getting at a hidden truth. In itself, of
course, there is nothing particularly wrong with his advise to use "indirections
[to] find directions out." But the nature of the truth which is to be found out by
these means is seriously inadequate. The truth is, for Polonius, a thing, a simple

object, which the sufficiently deceptive man ought to be able to sneak up on and seize. "Give me up the truth," he demands of Ophelia (I.iii.98), and (underscoring the worth of a truth negotiable in this manner) he tells Reynaldo to use a "bait of falsehood [to] take this carp of truth" (II.i.62). He can boast:

> If circumstances lead me, I will find
> Where truth is hid, though it were hid indeed
> Within the centre.
>
> (II.ii.156)

The truth in this case is the truth of Hamlet's motives, and it is appropriate that the sort of discovery the Polonian roundaboutness is able to make is itself a circularity:

> Mad call I it; for, to define true madness,
> What is't but to be nothing else but mad?
>
> (II.ii.93)

It is not, then, simply Polonius's habit of lurking behind arrases which is wrong. The mistake also comes in what he expects to find when he peeks from behind the arras onto the stage he has set. His belief in a unitary, capturable truth is in some ways similar to Hamlet's early belief in an inner core of essential being. But Polonius dies like a rat because he is too busy in his seeking to find anything; while Hamlet, both actor and observer of actors, learns a great lesson about ends and means: the hidden truth and the mode of discovery are one, Hamlet finds.

Polonius is not alone in his failings. Rosencrantz and Guildenstern also use dissembling to pluck out the heart of a mystery, and find that their acting only discovers an actor. Even those good soldiers on watch for the ghost in the opening scene were involved in the impossible search for answers to misstated questions. There is a lesson here for Hamlet, and one for us as well. When we approach the problem of Hamlet's delayed revenge—a problem more vexed than any ghost— and try to pluck out the heart of that mystery, we would do well to recall these epistemological muddles.

For are we not accustomed to thinking of Hamlet's task as Polonius thinks of truth—as something simple and unitary, capable of discovery although only, perhaps, after some initial indirectness? In fact, as I have tried to show, the act of revenge is conceived, by Hamlet and his creator, as an expressive act, a fully meaningful linguistic and gestural expression to be undertaken in a world where words and gestures have become largely meaningless. It is thus a creative as much as a destructive act, and is as complex and hard-won as all true acts of creation must be. To consider the question of Hamlet's delayed revenge in a narrower context is to run the risk of feeling cheated by the play. Hamlet, after all, never does consciously overcome whatever scruples or fastidiousness have kept him from his revenge;

rather he stumbles into it when the Claudius-Laertes plot misfires. Thus, a critic [Brents Stirling] can write that the duel, with all its attendant deaths, is mere "accident . . . which breaks the chain of motivation." But if not consciously willed, it is still no accident. Hamlet's protracted search for "revenge" is the search, not for mere action however bloody, but for fully expressive action. And what Hamlet finds is that this action must be accomplished as the players accomplish theirs, with the facing and fulfilling of the tragedy's necessary fifth act.

In *Feeling and Form,* Susanne Langer defines "the tragic rhythm" as "the pattern of a life that grows, flourishes, and declines." In tragedy, that universal life-rhythm "is abstracted by being transferred . . . to the sphere of characteristically human action, where it is exemplified in mental and emotional growth, maturation, and the final relinquishment of power." And, Langer adds, "In that relinquishment lies the hero's true 'heroism' — the vision of life as accomplished, that is, life in its entirety, the sense of fulfillment that lifts him above his defeat." To Hamlet, more perhaps than to any tragic hero except Oedipus, the search for the characteristic tragic rhythm becomes an almost self-conscious concern. Especially because of his interest in modes of playing, we are made to feel that Hamlet's quest (say, for revenge) is a quest for the shape of his own play, that Hamlet comes to recognize his subservience to the action, in the Aristotelian sense, for which he exists. Hamlet's task thus involves renunciation as well as action: that is the truth, both esthetic and existential, which he learns in part from his observation of the plays. "The readiness is all": in the tone of quiet acceptance which characterizes Hamlet in the play's closing moments we see the fruits of that observation.

An aspect of Hamlet's task has been to join the language of words to the proper language of gesture. And no gesture short of the final tragic gesture, Hamlet's death, will suffice. It is not only Claudius who must expiate the murder of old Hamlet, but Hamlet who must succeed a Hamlet as tragic victim. As the overdetermined image of Pyrrhus in the Player's speech suggests, avenger and victim must finally become one. Hamlet dies, and his death, the necessary end of his tragedy, enables his expressive gesture. Now to the living, to that steadfast and scholarly observer Horatio, falls the burden to report Hamlet and his cause aright. But then, Horatio's task has really been accomplished already, for (as Northrop Frye writes), "At the end of *Hamlet* we get a strong feeling that the play we are watching is, in a sense, Horatio's story." Hamlet achieves his necessary language with the completion, in death, when the time is ripe, of his tragic play. That language becomes ours, as it does Horatio's, to be delivered by us "aright / To the unsatisfied" (V.ii.331).

Superposed Plays

Richard A. Lanham

Shakespeare uses a variation on the sonnets strategy in *Hamlet*. He writes two plays in one. Laertes plays the revenge-tragedy hero straight. He does, true enough, veer toward self-parody, as when he complains that crying for Ophelia has interfered with his rants: "I have a speech o' fire, that fain would blaze / But that this folly drowns it" (IV.vii.189–90). But he knows his generic duty and does it. No sooner has his "good old man" (Polonius's role in the straight, "serious" play) been polished off than he comes screaming with a rabble army. He delivers predictably and suitably stupid lines like "O thou vile king, / Give me my father" (IV.v.115–16). And the Queen can scarcely manage a "Calmly, good Laertes" before he begins again:

> That drop of blood that's calm proclaims me bastard,
> Cries cuckold to my father, brands the harlot
> Even here between the chaste unsmirchèd brows
> Of my true mother.
>
> (IV.v.117–20)

And just before the King begins to calm him, to the villainous contentation of both:

> How came he dead? I'll not be juggled with.
> To hell allegiance, vows to the blackest devil,
> Conscience and grace to the profoundest pit!
>
> (IV.v.130–32)

He plays a straight, hard-charging revenge-hero.

From *The Motives of Eloquence: Literary Rhetoric in the Renaissance.* © 1976 by Yale University. Yale University Press, 1976. Originally entitled "Superposed Plays: *Hamlet.*"

Against him, Ophelia reenacts a delightfully tear-jerking madwoman stage prop. The King mouths kingly platitudes well enough ("There's such divinity doth hedge a king" [IV.v.123]), comes up with a suitably stagey, two-phase fail-safe plot, and urges the hero on ("Revenge should have no bounds"). And the whole comes suitably laced with moralizing guff. So the King plays a Polonius-of-the-leading-questions: "Laertes, was your father dear to you?" Laertes, with unusual common sense, returns, "Why ask you this?" And then the King is off for a dozen Polonian lines on love's alteration by time: "Not that I think you did not love your father, / But that I know love is begun by time" (IV.vii.109–10). Only then can he get back to, as he phrases it, "the quick o' th' ulcer." And the Queen plays out a careful scene on the brookside where Ophelia drowned. And wrestling in Ophelia's grave, Hamlet, annoyed at being upstaged by Laertes, protests, "I'll rant as well as thou." And, as superb finale, Laertes, at the fencing match, stands there prating about honor with the poisoned rapier in his hand. The poisoner-poisoned motif releases the Christian forgiveness that forgives us, too, for enjoying all that blood. *Hamlet* offers, then, a story frankly calculated to make the audience as well as the compositor run out of exclamation points.

Hamlet obligingly confesses himself Laertes' foil.

> In mine ignorance
> Your skill shall, like a star i'th'darkest night,
> Stick fiery off indeed.

It is the other way about, of course. Laertes foils for Hamlet. Shakespeare is up to his old chiasmatic business, writing a play about the kind of play he is writing. The main play overlaps as well as glossing the play criticized—again, a strategy of superposition. Polonius plays a muddling old proverb-monger, and a connoisseur of language, in the Hamlet play, as well as good old man in the Laertes play. Ophelia, though sentimental from the start, is both more naive and more duplicitous in the Hamlet play; and so with the King and Queen, too, both are more complex figures. Shakespeare endeavors especially to wire the two plots in parallel: two avenging sons and two dead fathers; brother's murder and "this brother's wager"; both Hamlet and Laertes in love with Ophelia; both dishonest before the duel (Hamlet pretending more madness than he displays when he kills Polonius), and so on.

Now there is no doubt about how to read the Laertes play: straight revenge tragedy, to be taken—as I've tried to imply in my summary—without solemnity. We are to enjoy the rants as rants. When we get tears instead of a rant, as with the Laertes instance cited earlier, an apology for our disappointment does not come amiss. We are not to be caught up in Laertes' vigorous feeling any more than in Ophelia's bawdy punning. We savor it. We don't believe the fake King when he maunders on about Divine Right, the divinity that doth hedge a king. We don't "believe" anybody. It is not that kind of play. For explanation, neither the ketchup nor the verbal violence need go further than enjoyment. The more outrageous the stage effects, the more ghastly the brutality, the more grotesque the physical mutilation, the better such a play becomes. Shakespeare had done this kind of thing already and knew what he was about. Such a vehicle packed them in. Just so, when part-sales were falling, would Dickens kill a baby.

The real doubt comes when we ask, "What poetic do we bring to the Hamlet play?" As several of its students have pointed out, it is a wordy play. Eloquence haunts it. Horatio starts the wordiness by supplying a footnote from ancient Rome in the first scene, by improving the occasion with informative reflection. Everybody laughs at Polonius for his moralizing glosses but Hamlet is just as bad. Worse. Gertrude asks him, in the second scene, why he grieves to excess and he gives us a disquisiton on seeming and reality in grief. The King follows with *his* bravura piece on grief. Everybody moralizes the pageant. The Hamlet play abounds with triggers for straight revenge-tragedy response. The whole "mystery" of Hamlet's hesitant revenge boils down to wondering why he doesn't go ahead and play his traditional part, complete with the elegant rants we know he can deliver.

The rhetorical attitude is triggered not only by obvious stylistic excess, as we have seen, or by *de trop* moralizing, but by talking about language, by surface reference to surface. This surface reference occurs at every level of the Hamlet play in *Hamlet,* as well as, of course, throughout the Laertes play. Polonius plays a main part here. His tedious prolixity ensures that we notice everyone else's tedious prolixity. And his relish of language, his speech for its own sake, makes us suspect the same appetite in others and in ourselves. The Queen's rejoinder to the marvelous "brevity is the soul of wit" speech in II.ii could be addressed to almost anybody in the play, including the gravedigger: "More matter, with less art."

Everyone is manipulating everyone else with speechifying and then admitting he has done so. Every grand rhetorical occasion seems no sooner blown than blasted. Polonius offers the famous Gielgud encore about being true to oneself and then sends off Reynaldo to spy and tell fetching lies. The King plays king to angry Laertes then confesses to Gertrude that he has been doing just this. Ophelia is staked out to play innocent maiden so Hamlet can be drawn out and observed. *Hic et ubique.* Is she a stage contrivance or a character? What kind of audience are we to be? Everyone is an actor, Hamlet and his madness most of all. The play is full of minor invitations to attend the surface, the theme of speaking. Even the ghost has to remind himself to be brief—before continuing for thirty-odd lines (I.v). Theatrical gestures are not simply used all the time but described, as in

Hamlet's inky cloak and windy suspiration for grief, or the costuming and gesture of the distracted lover, as the innocent Ophelia describes Hamlet's visit:

> My lord, as I was sewing in my closet,
> Lord Hamlet, with his doublet all unbraced,
> No hat upon his head, his stockings fouled,
> Ungartered, and down-gyvèd to his ankle,
> Pale as his shirt, his knees knocking each other,
> And with a look so piteous in purport
> As if he had been loosèd out of hell
> To speak of horrors—he comes before me.
>
> He took me by the wrist and held me hard.
> Then goes he to the length of all his arm,
> And with his other hand thus o'er his brow
> He falls to such perusal of my face
> As 'a would draw it. Long stayed he so.
> At last, a little shaking of mine arm
> And thrice his head thus waving up and down,
> He raised a sigh so piteous and profound
> As it did seem to shatter all his bulk
> And end his being. That done, he lets me go,
> And with his head over his shoulder turned
> He seemed to find his way without his eyes,
> For out o'doors he went without their helps
> And to the last bended their light on me.
>
> (II.i.77–84, 87–100)

This might have come from an actor's manual. Do we take it as such, respond as
professional actors?

The Hamlet play turns in on itself most obviously when the players visit.
Dramatic self-consciousness retrogresses a step further as the tragedians of the city
talk about themselves doing what they are just now doing in a play depicting
them doing just what. . . . The debate is about rightful succession, of course,
like both the Laertes and the Hamlet plays.

> What, are they children? Who maintains 'em? How are they escoted?
> Will they pursue the quality no longer than they can sing? Will they
> not say afterwards, if they should grow themselves to common players
> (as it is most like, if their means are no better), their writers do them
> wrong to make them exclaim against their own succession?
>
> (II.ii.338–44)

Who are the children in the "real" plays? Hamlet had invoked a typical cast a few lines earlier (314ff.) such as *Hamlet* itself uses and stressed that "he that plays the king shall be welcome." Hamlet will use the play, that is, *as a weapon*, the propaganda side of rhetorical poetic, to complement the Polonius-pleasure side. But before that, there is a rehearsal, for effect, to see whether the players are good enough to play the play within the play. Here, even more clearly than in the Laertes play, we confront the connoisseur's attitude toward language. Polonius supplies a chorus that for once fits: "Fore God, my lord, well spoken, with good accent and good discretion" (II.ii.454–55). This to Hamlet, a good actor, as Polonius was in his youth. They proceed in this vein, nibbling the words; "That's good. 'Mobled queen' is good."

The main question pressing is not, How does the feedback work? What relation is there, for example, between rugged Pyrrhus and Hamlet, or Laertes? Or what relation with the King, who also topples a kingdom? And why is Hamlet so keen to reach Hecuba? The main question is, How does all this connoisseurship affect the "serious" part of *Hamlet*? *Hamlet* is one of the great tragedies. It has generated more comment than any other written document in English literature, one would guess, reverent, serious comment on it as a serious play. Yet finally can we take *any* of its rhetoric seriously? If so, how much and when? The play is full of the usual release mechanisms for the rhetorical poetic. And, at the end, the Laertes play is there as stylistic control, to mock us if we have made the naive response. But what is the sophisticated response?

Hamlet focuses the issue, and the play, the plays, when he finally gets to Hecuba. He who has been so eager for a passionate speech is yet surprised when it comes and when it seizes the player:

> O, what a rogue and peasant slave am I!
> Is it not monstrous that this player here,
> But in a fiction, in a dream of passion,
> Could force his soul so to his own conceit
> That from her working all his visage wanned,
> Tears in his eyes, distraction in his aspect,
> A broken voice, and his whole function suiting
> With forms to his conceit? And all for nothing,
> For Hecuba!
> What's Hecuba to him, or he to Hecuba,
> That he should weep for her? What would he do
> Had he the motive and the cue for passion
> That I have?
>
> (II.ii.534–46)

Hamlet makes the point that dances before us in every scene. Dramatic, rhetorical motive is stronger than "real," serious motive. Situation prompts feeling in this play, rather than the other way round. Feelings are not real until played. Drama, ceremony, is always needed to authenticate experience. On the battlements Hamlet—with ghostly reinforcement—makes his friends not simply swear but make a big scene of it. Laertes keeps asking for *more ceremonies* for Ophelia's burial and is upset by his father's hugger-mugger interment. Hamlet plays and then breaks off ("Something too much of this") a stoic friendship scene with Horatio in III.ii. The stronger, the more genuine the feeling, the greater the need to display it.

The answer, then, to "What would he do . . . ?" is, presumably, "Kill the King!"? Not at all. "He would drown the stage with tears / And cleave the general ear with horrid speech" (II.ii.546–47). He would rant even better. And this Hamlet himself, by way of illustration, goes on to do:

> Yet I,
> A dull and muddy-mettled rascal, peak
> Like John-a-dreams, unpregnant of my cause,
> And can say nothing. No, not for a king,
> Upon whose property and most dear life
> A damned defeat was made. Am I a coward?
> Who calls me villain? breaks my pate across?
> Plucks off my beard and blows it in my face?
> Tweaks me by the nose? gives me the lie i'th'throat
> As deep as to the lungs? Who does me this?
> Ha, 'swounds, I should take it, for it cannot be
> But I am pigeon-livered and lack gall
> To make oppression bitter, or ere this
> I should ha' fatted all the region kites
> With this slave's offal. Bloody, bawdy villain!
> Remorseless, treacherous, lecherous, kindless villain!
> O, vengeance!
>
> (II.ii.551–67)

Hamlet is here having a fine time dining off his own fury, relishing his sublime passion. He gets a bit confused, to be sure: saying nothing is not his problem. If somebody did call him villain or pluck his beard it would be better, for his grievance would then find some dramatic equivalent, would become real enough to act upon. But he enjoys himself thoroughly. He also sees himself clearly, or at least clearly enough to voice our opinion of his behavior.

> Why, what an ass am I! This is most brave,
> That I, the son of a dear father murdered,
> Prompted to my revenge by heaven and hell,
> Must like a whore unpack my heart with words.
>
> (II.ii.568–71)

Hamlet is one of the most appealing characters the mind of man has ever created but he really is a bit of an ass, and not only here but all through the play. He remains incorrigibly dramatic. Do we like him because he speaks to our love of dramatic imposture? Because his solution, once he has seen his own posturing as such, is not immediate action but more playing?

> I'll have these players
> Play something like the murder of my father
> Before mine uncle.
>
> (II.ii.580–82)

Playing is where we will find reality, find the truth. The play works, of course, tells Hamlet again what he already knows, has had a spirit come specially from purgatory to tell him. But that is not the point. Or rather, that is the point insofar as this is a serious play. The rhetorical purpose is to sustain reality until yet another dramatic contrivance—ship, grave scene, duel—can sustain it yet further.

We saw in the sonnets [discussed elsewhere] how a passage can invoke opaque attitudes by logical incongruity. Something of the sort happens in the scene after this speech, the "To be or not to be" centerpiece. Plays flourish within plays here, too, of course. The King and Polonius dangle Ophelia as bait and watch. Hamlet sees this. He may even be, as W. A. Bebbington suggested, reading the "To be or not to be" speech from a book, using it, literally, as a stage prop to bemuse the spyers-on, convince them of his now-become-suicidal madness. No one in his right mind will fault the poetry. But it is irrelevant to anything that precedes. It fools Ophelia—no difficult matter—but it should not fool us. The question is whether Hamlet will act directly or through drama? Not at all. Instead, is he going to end it in the river? I put it thus familiarly to penetrate the serious numinosity surrounding this passage. Hamlet anatomizes grievance for all time. But does *he* suffer these grievances? He has a complaint indeed against the King and one against Ophelia. Why not do something about them instead of meditating on suicide? If the book is a stage prop, or the speech a trap for the hidden listeners, of course, the question of relevancy doesn't arise. The speech works beautifully. But we do not usually consider it a rhetorical trick. It is the most serious speech in the canon. But is it? It tells us nothing about Hamlet except what we already know—he is a good actor. Its relevance, in fact, may lurk just here. The real question by this point in the play is exactly this one: *Is* Hamlet or not? Or does he just act? What kind of self does he possess?

The whole play, we know, seeks authenticity, reality behind the arras, things as they are. Hamlet, we are to assume, embodies the only true self, the central self amidst a cast of wicked phonies. The play, seen this way, provided a natural delight for both the Victorians and the existentialists; their sentimentalism about the central self ran the same way. Yet the question really is whether Hamlet is *to be,* to act rather than reenact. Much has been written on the Melancholy-Man-in-the-Renaissance and how his problems apply to Hamlet. Much more has been written on Hamlet's paralysis. Yet, how irrelevant all this commentary is to the real problem, not *what* Hamlet's motive is but *what kind of* motive. Why can't he act? Angels and ministers of grace, he does nothing else. Polonius, Rosencrantz and Guildenstern, Laertes, Claudius, all go to it. But Hamlet never breaks through to "reality." His motives and his behavior remain dramatic from first to last. So, in spite of all those bodies at the end, commentators wonder if *Hamlet* amounts to a tragedy and, if so, what kind. Hamlet lacks the serious, central self tragedy requires. We are compelled to stand back, hold off our identification, and hence to locate the play within rhetorical coordinates, a tragicomedy about the two kinds of self and the two kinds of motive.

We see this theme in that second quarto scene (IV.iv) where Fortinbras and his army parade, with seeming irrelevance — at least to many directors, who cut it — across the stage. They parade so that Hamlet can reflect upon them. The theme is motive. The scene begins as a straightforward lesson in the vanity of human wishes. They go, the Captain tells Hamlet, "to gain a little patch of ground / That hath in it no profit but the name" (IV.iv.18–19). Hamlet seems to get the point, "the question of this straw," the absurd artificiality of human motive, and especially of aristocratic war, war for pleasure, for the pure glory of it. But then out jumps another non sequitur soliloquy:

> How all occasions do inform against me
> And spur my dull revenge! What is a man,
> In his chief good and market of his time
> Be but to sleep and feed? A beast, no more.
> Sure he that made us with such large discourse,
> Looking before and after, gave us not
> That capability and godlike reason
> To fust in us unused. Now, whether it be
> Bestial oblivion, or some craven scruple
> Of thinking too precisely on th' event —
> A thought which, quartered, hath but one part wisdom

And ever three parts coward—I do not know
Why yet I live to say, "This thing's to do,"
Sith I have cause, and will, and strength, and means
To do't.

(IV.iv.32–46)

What has reason to do with revenge? His question—why, with all his compelling reasons, doesn't he go on—is again well taken. Shakespeare has carefully given him the realest reasons a revenge hero ever had—father murdered, mother whored, kingdom usurped, his innocent maiden corrupted in her imagination. The answer to Hamlet's question marches about on the stage before him. As usual, he does not fully understand the problem. It is the Player King's tears all over again. Fortinbras's motivation is sublimely artificial, entirely dramatic. Honor. It has no profit in it but the name. Hamlet cannot act because he cannot find a way to dramatize his revenge. Chances he has, but, as when he surprises Claudius praying, they are not dramatic. Claudius is alone. To fall upon him and kill him would not be revenge, as he says, not because Claudius will die shriven but because he will not see it coming, because nobody is watching.

So, when Hamlet continues his soliloquy, he draws a moral precisely opposite to the expected one. Again, logical discontinuity triggers stylistic attitude:

Examples gross as earth exhort me.
Witness this army of such mass and charge,
Led by a delicate and tender prince,
Whose spirit, with divine ambition puffed,
Makes mouths at the invisible event,
Exposing what is mortal and unsure
To all that fortune, death, and danger dare,
Even for an eggshell. Rightly to be great
Is not to stir without great argument.
But greatly to find quarrel in a straw
When honor's at the stake. How stand I then,
That have a father killed, a mother stained,
Excitements of my reason and my blood,
And let all sleep, while to my shame I see
The imminent death of twenty thousand men
That for a fantasy and trick of fame
Go to their graves like beds, fight for a plot
Whereon the numbers cannot try the cause,
Which is not tomb enough and continent

> To hide the slain? O, from this time forth,
> My thoughts be bloody, or be nothing worth!
>   (IV.iv.46–66)

He sees but does not see. In some way, Fortinbras represents where he wants to go, what he wants to be, how he wants to behave. But he doesn't see how, nor altogether do we. If ever an allegorical puppet was dragged across a stage it is Fortinbras. Yet he haunts the play. His divine ambition begins the action of the play; he gets that offstage introduction Shakespeare is so fond of; he marches to Norway to make a point about motive; and he marches back at the end, inherits Denmark. Yet he stays cardboard. It is not real motive he represents but martial honor much rather.

Shakespeare sought to give *Hamlet* a pronounced military coloration from first to last. The play begins on guard; the ghost wears armor; Denmark is a most warlike state. Military honor is the accepted motive in a Denmark Fortinbras rightly inherits. Honor will cure what is rotten in Denmark, restore its proper values. Hamlet cannot set the times right because he cannot find in martial honor a full and sufficient motive for human life. Hamlet, says Fortinbras, would have done well had he been king, but we may be permitted to doubt it. He thinks too much. Yet honor and the soldier's life provide the model motive for *Hamlet*. All his working life, Shakespeare was fascinated and perplexed by how deeply the military motive satisfied man. It constituted a sublime secular commitment which, like the religious commitment, gave all away to get all back. Hamlet's self-consciousness keeps him from it, yes, but even more his search for real purpose. Chivalric war — all war, perhaps — is manufactured purpose. Hamlet can talk about clutching it to his bosom but he cannot do it, for there is nothing *inevitable* about it.

Military honor is finally a role, much like Laertes' role as revenge hero. Both roles are satisfying, both integrate and direct the personality. But once you realize that you are playing the role for just these reasons, using it as a self-serving device, its attraction fades. As its inevitability diminishes, so does its reality. War and revenge both prove finally so rewarding because they provide, by all the killing, the irrefutable reality needed to bolster the role, restore its inevitability. Thus Shakespeare chose them, a revenge plot superposed on a Fortinbras-honor plot, for his play about motive. They provided a model for the kind of motive men find most satisfying; they combine maximum dramatic satisfaction with the irrefutable reality only bloody death can supply. In the Elizabethan absurdity as in our own, men kill others and themselves because that is the only real thing left to do. It is a rare paradox and Shakespeare builds his play upon it.

But even death is not dependable. We can learn to make sport of it, enjoy it. So the gravedigger puns on his craft. So, too, I suppose, Fortinbras laconically remarks at the end of the play: "Such a sight as this / Becomes the field, but here shows much amiss." Death's reality can vanish too. All our purposes end up, like the skull Hamlet meditates on, a stage prop. It is not accidental that the language which closes the play is theatrical. Hamlet even in death does not escape the dramatic self. When the bodies are "high on a stage . . . placed to the view" Horatio will "speak to th' yet unknowing world," will authenticate the proceeding with a rhetorical occasion. Hamlet's body, Fortinbras commands, is to be borne

> like a soldier to the stage,
> For he was likely, had he been put on,
> To have proved most royal.

Nor is it accidental that Hamlet kills Polonius. The act is his real attempt at revenge, Polonius his real enemy. Polonius embodies the dramatic self-consciousness which stands between Hamlet and the roles — Avenger and King — he was born to play. But Polonius pervades the whole of Hamlet's world and lurks within Hamlet himself. Only death can free Hamlet. Perhaps this is why he faces it with nonchalance. Much as been said about Hamlet's stoicism, but how unstoical the play really is! Honest feeling demands a dramatic equivalent to make it real just as artifice does. Stoicism demands a preexistent reality, a central self beyond drama, which the play denies. Stoicism is death and indeed, in *Hamlet,* the second follows hard upon the avowal of the first. We have no choice but to play.

And so Hamlet chooses his foil and plays. I have been arguing that the play invokes rhetorical coordinates as well as serious ones. It makes sense, if this is so, that it should end with a sublime game and the triumph of chance. Hamlet never solves his problem, nor does chance solve it for him, nor does the play solve it for us. No satisfactory model for motive, no movement from game to sublime, is suggested. Hamlet can finally kill the King because the King thoughtfully supplies a dramatic occasion appropriate to the deed. And Hamlet can kill Laertes because dramatic motive has destroyed naive purpose. And vice versa. But Hamlet cannot get rid of his dramatic self, his dramatic motives. The duel allegorizes the quarrel between kinds of motive which the play has just dramatized. And the duel, like the play, is a zero-sum game. Interest for both sides adds up to zero. The play leaves us, finally, where it leaves Hamlet. We have savored the violence and the gorgeous poetry and been made aware that we do. We have been made to reflect on play as well as purpose. We have not been shown how to move from one to the other. Nor that it *cannot* be done. We are left, like those in the play, dependent on death and chance to show us how to put our two motives, our two selves, together.

Shakespeare as a mature playwright is not supposed to be an opaque stylist. The great unity of his mature tragedies is a style we look through, not at. The gamesman with words fades out with the nondramatic poems and early infatuations like *Love's Labor's Lost. Hamlet* shows, by itself, how wrong this view of Shakespeare's development is. The play depends upon an alternation of opaque and transparent styles for its meaning. The alternation almost *is* the meaning. *Hamlet* is a play about motive, about style, and thus perhaps, of the mature plays, an exception? I don't think so. Where Shakespeare is most sublime he is also most rhetorical and both poetics are likely to be present in force. To illustrate such a thesis would constitute an agreeable task. The lines it would follow are clear enough. They would yield explanation of the double plot more basic than the comic / serious one. They would render the comic / tragic division altogether less important than it now seems.

In play after play the same stylistic strategy illustrates the same juxtaposition of motive, of play and purpose. Richard cannot learn the difference. Hal must. Lear can play the king but he has never *been* a king. *Antony and Cleopatra* juxtaposes not only public and private life but two poetics and two selves. The double plot becomes, over and over, a serious plot-poetic and a play plot-poetic. The fatal innocence of Shakespeare's characters turns out, over and over, to be innocence about the real nature of their motivation. All through the *Henriad* political rhetoric must be *seen* as rhetoric. Egypt is meant to be *seen* as more wordy and more metaphorical than Rome. *Romeo and Juliet* depends on our seeing the Petrarchan rhetoric as such, else we will mistake the kind of play it is, a play where death authenticates game. Lear on the heath, that centerpiece of Shakespearean sublimity, alters his outlines considerably within rhetorical coordinates. Shakespearean tragedy may come to seem, as in *Hamlet,* a juxtaposition of the two motives with a hole in the middle, with no way to connect them. The comedies collapse them. And the problem plays and romances try to make a path between the two, see them in dynamic interchange. The two things that obsessed Shakespeare were style and motive, and his career can be charted coherently from beginning to end in terms of their interrelation. In this he typifies the stylistic strategy of the Renaissance as a whole. The real question of motive lay beyond good and evil. It was the principal task of the self-conscious rhetorical style to point this moral. Human flesh is sullied with self-consciousness, with theatricality, and these will be the ground for whatever authentic morality any of us can muster.

O'erdoing Termagant

Howard Felperin

> That was the old way, Gossip, when Iniquity came in like
> Hokos Pokos, in a Juglers jerkin, with false skirts, like the
> Knave of Clubs! but now they are attir'd like men and
> women o' the time, the Vices, male and female!
> BEN JOHNSON, *The Staple of News*,
> 2nd Intermean

There is probably no more promising point of departure for the study of Shake-speare's relation to his dramatic past than Hamlet's advice to the players:

> O, it offends me to the soul to hear a robustious periwig-pated fellow
> tear a passion to tatters, to very rags, to split the ears of the ground-
> lings, who (for the most part) are capable of nothing but inexplicable
> dumb shows and noise. I would have such a fellow whipp'd for o'er-
> doing Termagant. It out-herods Herod. Pray you avoid it. . . . Be
> not too tame neither; but let your own discretion be your tutor. Suit
> the action to the word, the word to the action; with this special ob-
> servance, that you o'erstep not the modesty of nature: for anything
> so overdone is from the purpose of playing, whose end, both at the
> first and now, was and is, to hold, as 'twere, the mirror up to nature;
> to show virtue her own feature, scorn her own image, and the very
> age and body of the time his form and pressure.
>
> (III.ii.7–25)

From *The Yale Review* 63, no. 3 (Spring 1974). © 1974 by Yale University. Originally entitled
"O'erdoing Termagant: An Approach to Shakespearean Mimesis."

At first glance, the speech seems perfectly straightforward and unambiguous. It begins with some practical pointers on acting and builds toward a general state-ment of the function of drama—one we would all readily agree with and quote often enough—which supports, in turn, the practical pointers. It evokes through many details an august tradition of classical and renaissance dramatic theory, and would seem to promote the kind of "modern" and "lifelike" drama we associate with Shakespeare at the expense of the old-fashioned and exaggerated drama we associate, often as a result of this speech, with the medieval stage. After all, Hamlet's discourse on the art of theater is, we like to say, the closest thing we have to a statement of Shakespeare's own aims and principles as a dramatist. Yet whether or not Hamlet's account of the purpose of playing is also Shakespeare's, the fact that it occupies a central place within the most theatrically self-conscious and complex of his plays makes it more problematic than is usually supposed, a text in certain respects ambiguous in its statement and inconsistent with the play that forms its context.

It is with the general statement of the function of drama that I am chiefly concerned here, both in its immediate application to *Hamlet* itself and in its wider implications for Shakespeare's work as a whole. In Hamlet's classic restatement of the commonplace—"to hold, as 'twere, the mirror up to nature"—the pur-pose of playing is twofold. Drama projects, on the one hand, a moral vision—"to show virtue her own feature, scorn her own image"—and on the other, a lifelike illusion—"the very age and body of the time his form and pressure." What Hamlet has done, in effect, is to conflate under the blanket phrase, "to hold the mirror up to nature," two distinct notions of drama, each with a long tradition and each in some degree antagonistic to the other in aim and method. The former, the view of the play as moral vision, transcends by its very nature considerations of time and place, associates drama with theology or moral philosophy, and is identifiable in Hamlet's account with medieval and Tudor allegorical theater— note the vestiges of personification in the phrases, "virtue *her own feature,* scorn *her own image.*" The latter, the view of the play as lifelike illusion, is by its very nature time-bound and localized, associates drama with historiography, and is identifiable in Hamlet's account with the more or less naturalistic theater of classical Rome and renaissance Italy. Taken as a whole, Hamlet's speech is pre-dominantly a plea for the new doctrine of dramatic illusionism and falls into line with the special pleading of such Elizabethan classicists as Sidney and Jonson. From such a point of view, to do Termagant at all is to overdo Termagant, for such roles as Termagant and Herod are written out of a homiletic rather than mimetic conception of drama, no matter how they were actually performed, in so far as they are offered as timeless and cautionary embodiments of wickedness and tyranny rather than as characterizations of human similitude. Moral images are not necessarily lifelike ones. But even though Hamlet's advice to the players stresses neoclassical decorum, the medieval conception of drama as a timeless moral vision, for all its apparent incompatibility, survives in it, as it does in the play of *Hamlet* itself.

For a specimen of that older dramatic mode we need look no further than the play-within-the-play. Hamlet describes it to Claudius as "the image of a murder done in Vienna: Gonzago is the duke's name; his wife, Baptista" (III.ii. 247–49); he stresses, that is, the play's naturalistic representation of an historical event enacted in a specific place by specific people. Any resemblance to persons living or dead in the Danish court, he implies, is purely coincidental. But this description of *The Murder of Gonzago* does not correspond to the play we see. Its alternative title *The Mousetrap,* which Hamlet calls it "tropically" or figuratively, is really much more accurate, for the play is "tropical" or figurative in its very conception, a piece of mirror-literature in the older sense, and might have been called *A Looking-Glass for Elsinore and Denmark,* a dramatic *exemplum* reflecting the moral essence of many historical situations, pre-eminently the present state of Denmark and its recent past. *The Murder of Gonzago* represents, in sum, the first phase of a typical revenge action of what might be termed the first wave, of the kind produced during the late 1580's and early 1590's when the form was still explicitly involved with the Tudor morality drama and its clear-cut personifications of virtue and vice. It opens with the archaic device of a dumb-show, which presents, not at all inexplicably, the murder of an idealized king and husband and the seduction of his queen by the treacherous usurper, who in the logic of this convention would then have met his own nemesis in the form of a revenger, with order and justice restored. ~~interrupt~~ *the real*

Within the interrupted performance we see, the player-king and queen have shed all literal identity as Gonzago and Baptista; the emblematic garden in which the player-king lies down has replaced any more or less historical Vienna as the play's setting; and the debate on marital fidelity, delivered in stylistically archaic end-stopped couplets and balanced rhetorical figures, works to generalize and depersonalize the situation out of which they speak. The characters themselves are wholly idealized, perfect embodiments of faith in love expressing exemplary attitudes as they strive with each other in "gentilesse." By naturalistic canons, the lady protests too much and too archaically to be believed. For a moment it might seem as if we had somehow blundered into one of John Heywood's moral interludes, until the entrance of Lucianus makes the play's revenge-orientation quite clear. From Hamlet's remarks upon Lucianus' entrance — "Pox, leave thy damnable faces, and begin! Come, the croaking raven doth bellow for revenge" (III.ii. 264–65) — we can assume that the actor who plays Lucianus is indulging in a good deal of the Tudor equivalent of mustachio-twisting, exploiting the theatricality implicit in the Vice's role. Hamlet's line on "the croaking raven" is actually quoted from a speech in the pre-Shakespearean *True Tragedy of Richard III* (printed 1594) spoken by Richard just at the point when his own nemesis, Henry of Richmond, is close at hand. The six lines that Lucianus, the counterpart of Richard in usurpation and seduction, has time to utter before Claudius, the counterpart of both within the world of *Hamlet,* breaks up the performance are in a vein familiar to students of those first-wave revenge plays—*The Spanish Tragedy, Soliman and Perseda, The True Tragedy of Richard III, Titus Andronicus,* and (dare I say it?) the *Ur-Hamlet:*

> Thoughts black, hands apt, drugs fit, and time agreeing;
> Confederate season, else no creature seeing;
> Thou mixture rank, of midnight weeds collected,
> With Hecate's ban thrice blasted, thrice infected,
> Thy natural magic and dire property
> On wholesome life usurp immediately.
>
> (III.ii.266–71)

At the very center of *Hamlet,* then, we have a substantial fragment of a primitive Elizabethan revenge tragedy, its morality affiliations—dumb-show, emblematic setting, generalizing rhetoric, virtue figures, and a highly theatrical Vice—intact. Like those older revenge plays, and revenge-plays-within-revenge-plays on which it is modeled, *The Murder of Gonzago* is by Hamlet's own standards archaic, conventional, and anti-mimetic. Of its dramatic mode in general we might well conclude that in this style it is impossible to tell the truth.

It would be convenient to think that in moving with Hamlet from the banquet hall of the play scene to his mother's closet we have also moved forward through theatrical history, left behind an archaic theatricality with its stiff and stylized postures for contemporary realism with its more intimate disclosures of deepest personality, and thereby taken the measure of Shakespeare's enormous advance on naturalism in the decade since his own *Titus Andronicus.* The only trouble is that the closet scene is in certain respects not less archaic and anti-mimetic than the play scene, but more so. Despite its attractiveness to nineteenth-century characterological and twentieth-century psychoanalytic critics, the closet scene tells us little about Hamlet's alleged state of mind. For most of the scene he does not speak as a son to his mother at all, but as a preacher to a sinner, not out of personal feeling but out of impersonal *indignatio.* His language and the role it expresses work to generalize, depersonalize, and archaize the scene out of all recognition as a naturalistic rendering of a son's mixed feelings toward his mother:

> Such an act
> That blurs the grace and blush of modesty,
> Calls virtue hypocrite, and takes the rose
> From the fair forehead of an innocent love
> And sets a blister there, makes marriage vows
> As false as dicers' oaths. O, such a deed
> As from the body of contraction plucks
> The very soul, and sweet religion makes
> A rhapsody of words! Heaven's face doth glow,
> And this solidity and compound mass,
> With heated visage, as against the doom,
> Is thought-sick at the act.
>
> (III.iv.41–52)

No medieval preacher ever inveighed against the horrors of incest, its assault upon the entire fabric of God's consecrated order, with greater homiletic inspiration than Hamlet does here. No wonder T. S. Eliot, his neo-classicism at that stage of his career stronger than his neo-medievalism, could find no "objective correlative" within the play for Hamlet's speeches. Even Gertrude vaguely perceives that Hamlet's speech is inspired more by ancient texts than by any immediate situation: "Ay me, what act, / That roars so loud and thunders in the index?" (III.iv.51–52) Here, as in so much of the play, we are confronted not with the ravings of a disordered personality but with the heroic frenzy of the prophet's role.

Moreover, Gertrude's terms are theatrical as well as bookish. They recall Hamlet's own caveats to the players about mouthing lines, tearing a passion to tatters, and splitting the ears of the groundlings. Surely at this moment Hamlet o'erdoes Termagant and out-herods Herod, o'ersteps the modesty of nature, and violates his own neoclassical doctrines of decorum in speech and action as flagrantly as the most unreformed ham among the tragedians of the city. In sum, Hamlet turns the stage during the closet scene into something closely akin to the older *theatrum mundi* of Termagant and Herod, as he recasts the experience of the play into a straightforward morality drama in which everyone has a clear-cut and conventional role:

> What devil was't
> That thus hath cozened you at hoodman-blind?
> Eyes without feeling, feeling without sight,
> Ears without hands or eyes, smelling sans all,
> Or but a sickly part of one true sense
> Could not so mope.

> Oh shame, where is thy blush? Rebellious hell,
> If thou canst mutine in a matron's bones,
> To flaming youth let virtue be as wax
> And melt in her own fire.
>
> (III.iv.77–86)

In Hamlet's rewriting of events, Gertrude is the misguided sinner related to the figure of hot-blooded youth, seduced by Vices like Will, Inclination, or Lust, in the moralities. Mary Magdalene, in the Digby play of that title, is a good example. Claudius is explicitly cast as such a Vice in Hamlet's morality, or rather as a composite Vice embodying several sins—lust, drunkenness, riot, etc.—right down to the details of his costume in pre-Shakespearean stage-tradition:

> A vice of kings,
> A cutpurse of the empire and the rule,
> That from a shelf the precious diadem stole
> And put it in his pocket. . . .
> A king of shreds and patches.
>
> (III.iv.99–103)

As for Hamlet himself, he takes on the role of a preacher, to be sure, specifically the chief virtue-figure of the morality, who tries to redeem the sinner from the snares of the Vice, usually, as Hamlet does here, by preaching him into repentance with Scriptural quotations and *exempla*, but often through a *coup de théâtre* like that of the two portraits of King Hamlet and Claudius, a device with many analogues in morality tradition. It recalls, for example, the picture of Wit in Redford's *Wit and Science* (c. 1531–47), which he no longer resembles after falling prey to the Vice, Idleness. When Wit incredulously looks into a glass held up by Reason, he finds himself all spotted and deformed. Gertrude's response to Hamlet's portrait-test underscores the parallel:

> Thou turn'st mine eyes into my very soul,
> And there I see such black and grained spots
> As will not leave their tinct.
>
> (III.iv.90–92)

Although Gertrude speaks figuratively here, her case had been literally represented on the medieval stage as far back as *Wisdom, Who Is Christ* (1461–85), where the fallen Anima "apperythe in the most horrybull wyse, fowlere than a fende" and is chastized into repentance by Wisdom: "Se howe ye have dysvyguryde yowr soule! / Beholde yowrselff; loke veryly in mynde!" (900–02). Throughout the scene, Hamlet holds the mirror up to nature in the same sense that a long line of preaching Virtues had done before him. "Forgive me this my virtue," he tells Gertrude, explicitly identifying himself with those older figures,

> For in the fatness of these pursy times
> Virtue itself of vice must pardon beg.
> Yea, curb and woo for leave to do him good.
> (III.iv.153–56)

His terms might be capitalized. Again they have the force and feel of personifications enacting a drama older than the play of *Hamlet,* older even than *The Murder of Gonzago.* What Hamlet has done in the closet scene is to cast the experience of the play into the dramatic mode of their common source, to rewrite *Hamlet* into a morality play.

The archaic aspect of *Hamlet,* though it is most conspicuous in the closet scene, is by no means confined to it but pervades the entire play. It enters *Hamlet* with the Ghost, not only the spirit of the elder Hamlet but in a sense the spirit of an older dramatic mode, whose account of recent events in Denmark is told from the eschatological point of view of the medieval drama: the "serpent" Claudius, having wrought King Hamlet's fall in his "orchard," proceeds under the figure of "lust" to "court" the "radiant angel" Gertrude "in a shape of heaven" and work her "falling-off" as well. Hamlet inherits not only his father's name, but his talent for writing morality plays. We could point out that the language in which Hamlet addresses Ophelia in the nunnery scene—"You jig, you amble, and you lisp" (III.i.150)—is not that of psychic derangement but of a preaching Virtue addressing a personification of Vanity or Lechery on the medieval stage. Or we could point to Claudius' account of his fratricide during his futile attempt to pray, a speech explicitly recalling the desperate utterances of Cain after he has murdered Abel in the mystery cycles. But these and other moments in *Hamlet* when the forms and figures of an older drama stand out from the more or less naturalistic surface of the play are really the tips of an iceberg or, more accurately, the protruding tusks of the mammoth preserved within it.

For it is nothing less than the revenge form itself that is archaic, not only in the sense I have already suggested, that the revenge play had been out of fashion for at least five years and just recently revived when Shakespeare turned to it again around 1600, but in a more fundamental sense as well. This deeper archaism is already implicit in some lines from *The Spanish Tragedy,* spoken by Hieronymo after he has conceived and cast his own revenge play-within-the-play and echoed by Hamlet after the success of *The Murder of Gonzago:*

> Now shall I see the fall of Babylon,
> Wrought by the heavens in this confusion.

> And if the world like not this tragedy,
> Hard is the hap of old Hieronymo.

Hieronymo, like Gertrude, might seem merely to speak figuratively, but his lines too reflect actual stage tradition. In the Protestant morality *Three Laws* (1530–36), for example, the figure of Vindicta Dei drives the chief Vice, Infidelity, off the stage with fire from heaven for what God calls his "Babylonical popery." In the Marian *Respublica* (1553), it is the figure of God's Nemesis who finally brings down judgment on the Protestant Vices, Avarice, Insolence, and Oppression, and restores the commonwealth to "tholde goode eastate." The figure of Divine Correction plays a similar role in Lindsay's *Satire of the Three Estates* (1535–40). In so far as the corrupt courts of the Elizabethan revenge plays are pseudohistorical counterparts to the typological Babylon, Sodom, and Gomorrah of medieval drama, its revenger-heroes are the natural and naturalized offspring of Vindicta Dei and God's Nemesis. Like Hieronymo, most Elizabethan revengers see themselves as scourges of God, legitimate heirs to those Virtue-figures who have divine authorization to commit whatever acts are required to set right the disjointed world, even if the command of a ghost is not quite the same thing as that of God. (A recent analogue is the "licence to kill" conferred on its agents by the modern state in the coldwar reincarnation of the medieval *psychomachia,* the spy novel.) From Hamlet's early assertion that "the time is out of joint: O cursed spite / That ever I was born to set it right" (I.v.189–90) to his parting remarks to his mother that

> Heaven hath pleas'd it so,
> To punish me with this, and this with me,
> That I must be their scourge and minister
> (III.iv.173–75)

he commits himself to a role and a form by their very nature anachronistic. Yet Hamlet's attempt to recast his experience into a morality play is actually half accomplished before he even begins, at least to the extent that the Elizabethan revenge play grows out of native morality tradition, a much greater extent than our preoccupation with Seneca would suggest.

There is, then, an important sense in which the legendary *Ur-Hamlet,* the crude old native play on the subject alluded to by Thomas Nashe and searched for in vain by generations of scholars, is very much alive in the midst of Shakespeare's *Hamlet.* This is not to suggest, however, that Shakespeare borrows nothing from English Seneca. On the contrary, Hamlet tries out classical roles for himself and those around him at several points in the play, but usually in such a way as to reveal their inappropriateness to his situation and rule them out as models for his own action. Gertrude, for example, is only too obviously unlike "Niobe, all tears," the type of the mourning queen to whom he ironically compares her, and Claudius is "no more like my father / Than I to Hercules," the paragon of heroic action. Even though the rugged Pyrrhus hesitates for an instant in the pseudo-Senecan speech, pregnant with present analogies, that Hamlet eagerly solicits from the chief player, whatever identification Hamlet may feel is effectively cancelled when Pyrrhus follows through with his regicide. Nor is this to suggest, however, that the native dramatic roles and forms that Hamlet finally falls back on and that seem to fit more comfortably are a perfect fit either. If they were, why would he continue to castigate himself with his own sense of unworthiness, of having so many offenses at his beck, even after he has cast himself in the self-righteous role of an avenging Virtue? As late as the final act, he is still attempting to close any remaining gap between himself and his chosen role, even as the rhetorical nature of that attempt calls attention to the gap and puts into question the propriety of the role:

> Does it not, think thee, stand me now upon . . .
>   is't not perfect conscience
> To quit him with this arm?
> And is't not to be damned
> To let this canker of our nature come
> In further evil?
>
>   (V.ii.63–70)

Clearly Hamlet knows at some level that he is not and can never become the potent abstraction acting out of lofty and impersonal motives that he makes himself out to be, any more than his experience can wholly conform, or be made to conform, to the older scenario of just and perfect vengeance that he tries to turn it into.

At this point in our discussion we seem to be verging upon an older approach to the classic problem of incoherence and archaism in *Hamlet,* the one exemplified by T. S. Eliot in his well-known essay on the subject. There, Eliot postulates a Shakespeare "unable to impose this motive [of the effect of a mother's guilt upon her son] successfully upon the 'intractable' materials of the old play" and a *Hamlet* "superimposed upon much cruder material which persists even in the final form," a play, in sum, that is "most certainly an artistic failure." Eliot's unhappy judgments are worth considering here, if only because they are based on an intuition of Shakespeare's creative process that is so near to and yet so far from the one presupposed in the present essay. He imagines Shakespeare grappling with his archaic sources in the attempt to naturalize, rationalize, and psychologize—generally speaking, to streamline and neoclassicize them—and at least in the case of *Hamlet,* losing the struggle. Our own intuition of the creative or re-creative act that issued in the play also assumes a struggle with the literary past, but one of a more complex nature. It would seem to be Hamlet who is unable to impose successfully the model of an old play upon the intractable material of his present life, and Shakespeare who dramatizes with unfailing control the tragic conflict between his heroic effort to do so and his ironic consciousness that it cannot be done, with the inevitable by-products of hesitation and delay. Hamlet may well be a projection of Shakespeare's creative self, but there is no doubt as to which is *il miglior fabbro*. After all, if this be failure, what in the world of the arts constitutes success?

For even in those Shakespearean plays for which there are no lost ur-versions, we still encounter a no less pervasive archaism and a scarcely less notorious incoherence by naturalistic or neoclassical standards. Iago, for example, whose motives for doing what he does have proved almost as elusive as Hamlet's for not doing what he is supposed to do, emerges from Bernard Spivack's study of the "hybridization" of allegorical and naturalistic drama in the sixteenth century as your old Vice still, hating and intriguing according to conventions older than those which dominate *Othello* as a whole. And Maynard Mack has reformulated the longstanding problem of staging *King Lear* in terms of the conflicting dramatic worlds the play simultaneously inhabits, the one medieval and visionary and the other modern and illusionistic. If the archaism informing *Hamlet* makes it an artistic failure, so too are *Othello* and *Lear*.

The archeological research into Shakespeare's background in the morality plays pioneered by Spivack has taken us well beyond the genetic speculations culminating in Eliot. Perhaps not surprisingly, however, the poet-critic Eliot seems to approach more closely to Shakespeare's creative process than do these more recent scholars. For their work hardly envisions or requires a creative act at all, based as it is on certain misleading assumptions concerning the "evolution" of dramatic forms which derive, in turn, from the theory of the evolution of biological forms, and trail clouds of imagery whence they came. Spivack in particular talks of "hybrid" plays and characters, of "the complex pregnancy of the Elizabethan drama," of how "the great organism [of Shakespeare's work] unfolds its successive stages of maturity," and, most tellingly, of "survivals of the older subject and the older technique" into Shakespearean drama. The implicit evolutionary analogy is misleading in so far as it infers from the fact of change a large, impersonal, and inexorable force of change, a spirit of naturalism which, like the spirit of nature in Wordsworth, rolls through all things and irresistibly transforms the Elizabethan drama. Except, that is, for certain survivals, vestiges, or fossils that linger on, inert but not annihilated. In such accounts of the "evolution" of the drama, as in its Darwinian counterpart, the individual *qua* individual is less important than the species: he is the unwitting medium through whom change manifests itself; his options are to adapt or die, hardly options at all. Little allowance is made in Spivack's or other accounts for what might be termed creative evolution, the capacity of the individual to exercise control over the rate and direction of his own adaptation. For the simple fact is that not all contemporary playwrights are equally archaic or naturalistic. The relation of the individual talent, especially though not exclusively a talent the size of Shakespeare's, to available tradition remains unresolved.

The archaic content of Shakespeare's work is vast but, at least as far as we have seen in the case of *Hamlet,* not haphazard. It remains to be demonstrated that virtually any of his plays will yield, on scrutiny, not a wide scattering of fossilized bones and teeth from an earlier era but the almost perfectly preserved mammoth similar to the one we have begun to disinter. One reason I have chosen *Hamlet* as a point of departure, a play usually discussed in terms of revenge — as distinct from morality — tradition, is incidentally to show that *Othello* and *Lear* are not exceptional in their rich and complex relation to morality tradition. They are not special cases, as they have been generally regarded, but typical cases. Moreover, if archaism in Shakespeare were simply an untransmuted residue left behind by the ever-encroaching tide of naturalism, we should expect to encounter more fossils at the beginning of his twenty-year career than at the end. If anything, the opposite is the case: the final romances are now generally recognized to be *more,* not less, archaic than the early comedies. Similarly, the morality skeleton often observed in *Henry IV* of a darkened prince of the world flanked by the Virtues of honor and justice and the reverend Vices of riot and debauchery is no less visible, though less often noticed, in *Antony and Cleopatra.* In its large outline and certain local details, Richard III's career recalls the rise and fall of several tyrants and child-murderers of the medieval stage — Pharoah, Herod, Cambyses — but so does Macbeth's. *Richard II* can be seen as one more sad story of the death of kings, a medieval *exemplum* of the educative abasement of the high and mighty not unlike those of *A Mirror For Magistrates;* but so too can *King Lear.* This last example suggests a final criticism of Spivack's approach and the starting-point for a new one. In *Richard II,* there is a great deal in the way of scriptural parallels, medieval pageantry, and emblematic scenes and *tableaux,* but most of it radiates outward, as it were, from Richard's own characterization. He is the immediate author of his play's archaic theatricality, as when he stage-manages the challenge at Coventry, compares himself to Christ and his minions to Judases, calls for a looking-glass during his deposition, and so on. We should distinguish, as neither Eliot nor Spivack does, between that archaism which is Shakespeare's and that archaism which is Richard's or Falstaff's or the elder Hamlet's or Hamlet's own. For Shakespeare often surrounds a character with the trappings of an archaic theatricality as a way of identifying him with an older and passing order of things.

The evidence suggests that Shakespeare, far from being an unwitting medium of theatrical change through whose pen archaism and naturalism flow in proportions varying with the date of a given play, is rather the deliberate mediator of theatrical change, concentrating his archaism at certain strategic points, fully aware of the outmodedness of the forms and figures at his disposal.

Given so high a degree of self-awareness, independence, and discrimination in Shakespeare's use of older modes, it is conceivably within his power to purge his plays of all archaism and give them over altogether to the new naturalism; yet he chooses not to do so. It takes not a Shakespeare to do that but a Beaumont and Fletcher. Instead, Shakespeare does something more truly sophisticated. He invalidates older modes even as he includes them, supersedes them, in the very act of subsuming them. The result is a troubled awareness, shared by Hamlet himself, of the simultaneous resemblance and discrepancy between the play and its older models that is increasingly forced upon us as the action proceeds. In *The Murder of Gonzago,* the archaic center of *Hamlet,* we watch Shakespeare's play approach and embrace, as it were, its own archaic prototype, only to turn and flee it in an almost choreographic pattern of meeting and parting. Hamlet has selected the old play from the repertory of the tragedians of the city for its mirror-relation to the Danish court and inserted "some dozen or sixteen lines" to sharpen that relation. Yet this "knavish piece of work," as Hamlet terms it, with its dumb-show, idealized characters, and grimacing villain right out of the "croaking raven" school of revenge melodrama, seems less than promising as a mirror or model of the Danish court. Its sheer staginess, its dramaturgic and stylistic archaism, separate it widely from the life of Denmark that frames and mocks it. Then, suddenly, Claudius catches his reflection in its cracked and faded glass, and *The Murder of Gonzago* dissolves into Hamlet, becomes for a while indistinguishable from it.

The play is successful beyond even Hamlet's expectations, as almost everyone assumes the role prescribed for him by this older drama. Hamlet throws himself wholeheartedly into the stock and stagy role of Nemesis, of latter-day Vindicta Dei, and delivers a bloodthirsty soliloquy very much in Lucianus' vein:

> 'Tis now the very witching time of night,
> When churchyards yawn, and hell itself breathes out
> Contagion to this world. Now I could drink hot blood.
>
> (III.ii.406 ff)

Settling deeper into this self-righteous role, he proceeds to horrify Samuel Johnson with another soliloquy in which he "contrives damnation for the man he would punish," the godlike office he later executes on Rosencrantz and Guildenstern. He confronts his mother with her prescribed role of fallen but redeemable sinner, which she reluctantly takes on but promises to play out by mending her ways. Claudius meanwhile fulfills his assigned role of unregenerate Vice, and cursed Cain, by admitting his crimes and failing in his effort to pray. Even Ophelia casts herself as a latter-day Patient Griselda, the role taken in the subsequent tragedies by Desdemona and Cordelia, the wronged Virtue who must suffer long and be kind, love and be silent, while she waits for her beloved to wake from his madness. The archaic model roughed out by the Ghost, made flesh in *The Murder of Gonzago,* and refined by Hamlet seems for a while adequate to contain the experience of the play.

Yet all these older roles, and the form that adumbrates them, are already beginning to split at the seams under the pressure of events by the time Hamlet embarks for England. By the time he returns, they have all but burst apart. For one thing, Claudius' impulse to pray, to repent of his sins, distinguishes him from those older embodiments of wickedness who were constitutionally unable to do so. This merely confirms something we had suspected all along, for Claudius is never presented to us as the loathesome degenerate Hamlet makes him out to be. (He never appears on-stage drunk, and is far from a groping satyr in his dealings with Gertrude.) Hamlet, in turn, has failed to see that Claudius cannot pray, and thereby misses his chance for revenge; still worse, he goes on to kill the wrong man. The older figure of Vindicta Dei would not have made either mistake, could not have been deceived by appearances as Hamlet has been, for he lived and moved and had his being in a dramatic mode that truly knew not "seems," a world of moral absolutes, of essential reality, in which God's vengeance could not swerve from its proper object. Moreover, by killing Polonius Hamlet has raised his own Nemesis in Laertes, who embraces the role of fire-breathing revenger with more passion but less theatrical skill and moral discrimination than Hamlet. Meanwhile, Patient Griselda has gone mad; she cannot sustain her part. To adapt a phrase from an Ibsen play well to the other side of naturalism, "people don't do such things" in morality plays, but then, that is because they are not presented as people, whose psyches can crack and who take on roles for which they are ill-suited. In the medieval drama there is no gap between the role and the character; the role *is* the character. In *Hamlet,* in Shakespeare, the role and the identity that assumes it are separable, and characters choose roles they cannot play or play well. Such unforeseen repercussions, casualties, and miscalculations would not have occurred in a morality, and few of them in an early revenge play. There, expectation is still governed by recognized convention, and murder, however bloody or grotesque, goes by design. In the more circumstantial world of *Hamlet,* with its "accidental judgments, casual slaughters . . . , purposes mistook / Fall'n on th'inventors' heads" (V.ii.393–96), the conventions and expectations of that programmatic world exist only to be frustrated.

In the Hamlet who returns from his accident-filled and abortive voyage to England, and who talks quietly with Horatio in the hall, awaiting what the interim will bring, many commentators have seen a changed Hamlet. Perhaps one measure of the change in Hamlet is his repudiation of the role in which he had formerly cast himself:

> Let us know,
> Our indiscretion sometime serves us well
> When our deep plots do pall; and that should learn us
> There's a divinity that shapes our ends,
> Rough-hew them how we will.
>
> (V.ii.7–11)

The older model into which he has tried to cast the experience of the play has broken down completely. That model was originally designed to comprehend the essential reality above or behind the world of appearances in which we live, which from its point of view is sheer illusion. Hamlet lives and dies knowing only "seems"; only God knows "is." In Hamlet's hands, the older model has proved rough-hewn indeed. His efforts to fit the life of Denmark into it have come increasingly to resemble those of the sorcerer's apprentice, or in his own phrase for bad actors, one of "Nature's journeymen," as this self-styled Virtue is indictable by the end of the play for a series of offences ranging from breach of promise through involuntary manslaughter to premeditated murder. The metaphoric "license to kill" of the old figure of Vindicta Dei has long since expired in a dramatic world in which representation entails a fall into interpretation and subjectivity. The protagonist of *Horestes* (1567), first of Elizabethan revengers, is also the last to hold such a license, and even he has trouble qualifying for it. Revengers, in their human fallibility, are now doomed to be hero-villains. The metaphoric license to kill could exist only in a dramatic mode itself a sacred metaphor. Hamlet's attempt to re-enact such a role in a world in which all metaphor is poetic and therefore problematic had been an error of theatrical and moral anachronism. He has tried to be a two-dimensional character in a three-dimensional world.

Throughout the final act Hamlet does his best to salvage the morality play he has vainly tried to shape. From the *danse macabre* of the graveyard scene, where kings and clowns, lawyers and gentlewomen mingle indecorously in Hamlet's imagination, to the summoning by death at the end, he mitigates the severity of his earlier vision and earlier role. Against these latest paradigms, the incongruities of that self-righteous posture, now re-enacted by Laertes, become such stuff as parodies are made on. But even in his closing speeches Hamlet does not so much purge himself of all histrionic and directorial impulses—no Shakespearean character ever changes completely — as exchange one archaic model for another, a heroic for a humble role, Vindicta Dei for Everyman:

> You that look pale and tremble at this chance,
> That are but mutes or audience to this act,
> Had I but time (as this fell sergeant, Death,
> Is strict in his arrest) O, I could tell you —
> But let it be. Horatio, I am dead:
> Thou liv'st; report me and my cause aright
> To the unsatisfied.
>
> (V.ii.345–51)

Horatio, always the good scholar, picks up Hamlet's allusion and carries it to its logical conclusion: "Good night, sweet prince, / And flights of angels sing thee to thy rest!" (V.ii.370–71). But in likening Hamlet's death to the salvation of the morality protagonist, perhaps Horatio presses the analogy too far. For it is his *secular* salvation that concerns Hamlet, the "wounded name" that survives him in history. The other world of the morality drama recedes into a purer kind of dumb-show where "silence" reigns. It is within the historical appearances of "this harsh world" that his story will be weighed and he judged. The play leaves behind its final archaic model by ending on a this-worldly note.

Critics still argue over whether Hamlet is finally a hero or a villain, whether Othello in his last great speech asserts Christian humility or heathen bravado, whether Lear dies illuminated or deceived, and whether Macbeth's death "becomes" him in a fair or foul sense. Such questions are central and crucial to the plays that raise them and reflect what is usually called Shakespeare's characteristic balance and ambiguity. No doubt they represent a refinement beyond the days when critics argued about the afterlives of Shakespeare's heroes, but they proceed, I believe, from the same source within the plays. Though I can offer no definitive answers to these questions, I think we are in a better position now to see why they arise in the first place. They arise, I submit, because the older models embedded in the plays cast life as a drama of salvation and damnation, and the repudiation of those older models guarantees that there will be no clear-cut cases of salvation and damnation. The older models raise the questions; their repudiation insures a multiplicity of responses to them. Shakespeare's plays inhabit the gap between things and the preordained meaning of things, between experience and inherited constructs of experience. Edgar's injunction at the end of *King Lear* to "speak what we feel, not what we ought to say" formulates the difference between our responses to the drama of naturalism and the drama of allegory, and might serve as rubric to the history of Shakespeare criticism. We must speak what we feel because Shakespeare's plays no longer dictate what we ought to say; they offer merely cues, hints, signs. Out of the friction between life and the older models designed to contain life is generated not only the heat of critical controversy but the light of Shakespearean meaning.

Just as the study of his "modernity" begins in the study of his literary past, the study of Shakespearean mimesis, surely the most compelling illusion of reality in world literature, begins paradoxically in the study of convention. Any artist, in order to represent life, must resort to the conventions of art, and in so doing, falsify life in so far as art creates a world rival to life's. Yet for art to be moral, to teach as well as delight, it must also be mimetic; we cannot learn from the actions of creatures with whom we have nothing in common, who are not in some degree like us. Shakespeare resolves this paradox by subsuming within his work a recognizably conventional model of life, repudiating that model, and thereby creating the illusion that he uses no art at all, that he is presenting life directly. Of course what he is really presenting is a more complicated model with its own conventions — one of which is the breakdown of convention — a model that, to adopt Samuel Johnson's phrase, opens an appeal from convention to nature. One reverend Vice of the moralities is a coward, that is, he is Cowardice who masquerades as Courage. Falstaff is like this Vice; yet he is also, as Shakespeare makes equally clear, unlike this Vice in so far as he expresses a range of emotion well beyond that of an allegorical abstraction. Critics can then bring to bear on him their various codes of cowardice and courage in this world in the effort to denote him more truly, some concluding that he is, others that he is not, a coward. The important point, however, is that we half-perceive and half-create Falstaff. The miracle of Shakespearean characterization depends finally, not on his modeling his characters on people he knew, but on his opening up inherited dramatic models to invite, even demand, other models of understanding, including those we use on people we know.

It might be objected that, except by spending a lot of time in libraries, we cannot know the older conventions of character and action from which Shakespeare creatively departs, and therefore cannot recognize those departures and respond to the new meanings they make possible. This is clearly not the case, however, since those older models are not only stored away in libraries but are carried around, as it were, within the plays themselves, and are there to be perceived by the learned and unlearned alike. The most cursory acquaintance with the tradition of Shakespearean interpretation will turn up ample evidence of the naive identification of the play with its models by the most learned scholars, of the failure to perceive its implicit critique of and departure from those models. And those of us who teach will acknowledge that relatively unlearned students are capable of highly sophisticated distinctions between conventional and unconventional language and conduct within the same play. More often than not, however, these naive and sophisticated responses will co-exist within the same reader, and the process of literary education may well be one of sophisticating our naive responses while keeping in touch with them, of developing a sophisticated simplicity of response that mirrors the sophisticated simplicity of literature. This process will go on whether or not we can name the *de casibus* tragedy or revenge melodrama of the first wave encoded within the play that triggers our naive response in the first place, for it is nothing other than the process of interpretation itself. But the literary-historical knowledge that enables us to do so is an invaluable asset to interpretation, since it provides a means of subjecting to fuller and more rigorous scrutiny responses that might otherwise remain intuitive, impressionistic, and unexamined.

Reforming the Role

Mark Rose

Classical and Elizabethan tragedy represent polar opposites in dramatic structure, the one tightly focused with few characters and a sharply defined action, the other loose and sprawling with many characters, multiple locales, and complex plots which may span years of narrative time. And yet all tragedies tend to share certain central concerns. Sophocles' Oedipus fled Corinth to prevent the oracle's prophecy from coming true, but in the process of trying to escape his fate he only succeeded in fulfilling it. Sophocles' play is concerned, we might say, with the degree to which our lives are not in our own control. The words of the player king in *Hamlet* are apposite:

> Our wills and fates do so contrary run
> That our devices still are overthrown;
> Our thoughts are ours, their ends none of our own.
> (III.ii.217–19)

Hamlet, too, is concerned with the limits imposed upon mortal will, with the various restrictions that flesh is heir to; and it is upon this central tragic theme that I wish to dwell, suggesting how Shakespeare employs a characteristically Renaissance self-consciousness to transmute a popular Elizabethan dramatic form, the revenge play, into a tragedy the equal of Sophocles'.

Early in the play Polonius speaks to Ophelia of the "tether" with which Hamlet walks. The image is a useful one to keep in mind, for it suggests both that the prince does have a degree of freedom and that ultimately he is bound.

From *Homer to Brecht: The European Epic and Dramatic Traditions,* edited by Michael Seidel and Edward Mendelson. © 1977 by Yale University. Yale University Press, 1977. Originally entitled "Hamlet."

Laertes cautions Ophelia in a similar manner and develops more explicitly the limits on Hamlet's freedom. The prince's "will is not his own," Laertes says,

> For he himself is subject to his birth,
> He may not, as unvalued persons do,
> Carve for himself; for on his choice depends
> The safety and the health of this whole state.
>
> (I.iii.18–21)

What Laertes means is simply that Hamlet as heir apparent may not be free to marry Ophelia, but he says much more than he realizes. Hamlet is indeed subject to his birth, bound by being the dead king's son, and upon his "carving"— his rapier and dagger-work—the safety and health of Denmark do literally depend. Possibly Shakespeare has in mind the imagery of *Julius Caesar* and Brutus's pledge to be a sacrificer rather than a butcher, to carve Caesar as a dish fit for the gods, for, like Brutus, Hamlet is concerned with the manner of his carving. But the word is also Shakespeare's term for sculptor, and perhaps he is thinking of Hamlet as this kind of carver, an artist attempting to shape his revenge and his life according to his own standards. Yet here, too, Hamlet's will is not his own: there is, he discovers, "a divinity that shapes our ends, / Rough-hew them how we will" (V.ii.10–11).

From the first scene in which the prince appears, Shakespeare wishes us to perceive clearly that Hamlet is tethered. He contrasts the king's permission to Laertes to return to France with his polite refusal of Hamlet's request to return to Wittenberg. Denmark is in fact a prison for Hamlet, a kind of detention center in which the wary usurper can keep an eye on his disgruntled stepson. Claudius acclaims Hamlet's yielding as "gentle and unforced" and announces that he will celebrate it by firing his cannon to the heavens, but what he has done in fact is to cut ruthlessly the avenue of escape that the prince had sought from a court and a world he now loathes. One other, more desperate avenue still seems open, and as soon as the stage is cleared the prince considers the possibility of this course, suicide, only to remind himself that against this stands another sort of "canon," one fixed by God. Hamlet is tied to Elsinore, bound by his birth; on either side the road of escape is guarded and all that remains to him is his disgust for the world and the feeble wish that somehow his flesh will of itself melt into a puddle.

Hamlet's real prison is of course more a matter of mental than physical space. "Oh God," he exclaims to Rosencrantz and Guildenstern, "I could be bounded in a nutshell and count myself a king of infinite space, were it not that I have bad dreams" (II.ii.258–60). The erstwhile friends suppose Hamlet means he is ambitious for the crown, but the bad dream the prince is thinking of, the insubstantial "shadow" as he calls it, is evidently the ghost and its nightmarish revelation. If Claudius has tied him to Elsinore it is of little consequence compared to the way the ghost has bound him to vengeance. Hamlet's master turns out to be even a more formidable figure than the king. Ironically, Laertes' and Polonius's remarks upon what they conceive to be the limits placed upon Hamlet's freedom immediately precede the scene in which the prince at last encounters the ghost and discovers what it means to be subject to one's birth. "Speak," Hamlet says to the ghost, "I am bound to hear," and the ghost in his reply picks up the significant word *bound* and throws it back at the prince: "So art thou to revenge, when thou shalt hear" (I.v.6–7). Hamlet cannot shuffle off his father's spirit any more than he can the mortal coil. The ghost's command is "Remember me," and after his departure Shakespeare dramatizes how from this charge there is no escape. Hamlet rushes about the stage seeking a place to swear his companions to secrecy, but wherever he makes his stand the ghost is there directly — "Hic et ubique," the prince says — its voice crying from the cellarage: "Swear!"

The ghost binds Hamlet to vengeance, but there is another and more subtle way in which the spirit of his father haunts the prince. It is one of the radical ironies of the tragedy that the same nightmarish figure who takes from Hamlet his freedom should also embody the ideal of man noble in reason and infinite in faculties — the ideal of man, in other words, as free. The ghost of King Hamlet, stalking his son dressed in the same armor he wore in heroic combat with Fortinbras of Norway, becomes a peripatetic emblem of human dignity and worth, a memento of the time before the "falling-off" when Hamlet's serpent-uncle had not yet crept into the garden, infesting it with things rank and gross in nature. It is no accident that Hamlet bears the same name as his father: the king represents everything to which the prince aspires. Hamlet, too, has his single-combats, his duels both metaphorical and literal, but the world in which he must strive is not his father's. The memory of those two primal, valiant kings, face to face in a royal combat ratified by law and heraldry, haunts the tragedy, looming behind each pass of the "incensed points" of the modern "mighty opposites," Hamlet and Claudius, and looming also behind the final combat, Hamlet's and Laertes' poisoned play, swaddled in a show of chivalry as "yeasty" as the eloquence of Osric, the waterfly who presides as master of the lists.

Subject to his birth, tethered by Claudius, and bound by the ghost, Hamlet is obsessed with the idea of freedom, with the dignity that resides in being master of oneself. One must not be "passion's slave," a "pipe for Fortune's finger / To sound what stop she please" (III.ii.72–74) — nor for that matter a pipe for men to play. The first three acts are largely concerned with the attempts of Claudius and Hamlet to play upon each other, the king principally through Rosencrantz and Guildenstern, Hamlet through "The Mousetrap." It is Hamlet who succeeds, plucking at last the heart of Claudius's mystery, pressing the king to the point where he loses his self-control and rises in a passion, calling for light. "Dids't perceive?" Hamlet asks, and Horatio replies: "I did very well note him" (III.ii.293, 296). I should like to see a musical pun in Horatio's word *note*, but perhaps it is farfetched. At any rate, Hamlet's immediate response is to call for music, for the recorders to be brought, as if he thinks to reenact symbolically his triumph over the king. What follows is the "recorder scene" in which Rosencrantz and Guildenstern once again fail with Hamlet precisely where he has succeeded with the king:

> Why, look you now, how unworthy a thing you make of me!
> You would play upon me; you would seem to know my stops; you
> would pluck out the heart of my mystery; you would sound me from
> my lowest note to the top of my compass; and there is much music,
> excellent voice, in this little organ, yet cannot you make it speak.
> 'Sblood, do you think I am easier to be played on than a pipe? Call
> me what instrument you will, though you can fret me, you cannot
> play upon me.

(III.ii.371–80)

Immediately after speaking this, Hamlet turns to Polonius, who has just entered, and leads the old courtier through the game of cloud shapes, making him see the cloud first as a camel, then as a weasel, and finally as a whale. Though Claudius and his instruments cannot play upon him, Hamlet is contemptuously demonstrating that he can make any of them sound what tune he pleases.

Hamlet's disdain for anyone who will allow himself to be made an instrument perhaps suggests his bitter suspicion that he, too, is a kind of pipe. One of the most interesting of the bonds imposed upon Hamlet is presented in theatrical terms. Putting it baldly and exaggerating somewhat for the sake of clarity, one might say that Hamlet discovers that life is a poor play, that he finds himself compelled to play a part in a drama that offends his sense of his own worth. Hamlet is made to sound a tune that is not his own, the whirling and passionate music of the conventional revenger, a stock character familiar to the Elizabethans under a host of names, including Thomas Kyd's Hieronomo, his Hamlet, and Shakespeare's own Titus Andronicus. The role of revenger is thrust upon Hamlet by the ghost, and once again it is profoundly ironic that the figure who represents the dignity of man should be the agent for casting his son in a limited, hackneyed, and debasing role. That Hamlet should be constrained to play a role at all is a restriction of his freedom, but that it should be this particular, vulgar role is especially degrading.

Lest I should seem to be refashioning Shakespeare in the modern image of Pirandello, let me recall at this point that he is a remarkably self-conscious playwright, one who delights in such reflexive devices as the play within the play, the character who is either consciously or unconsciously an actor, or the great set speech on that favorite theme of how all the world is a stage. Of all Shakespeare's plays, perhaps the most reflexive, the most dramatically self-conscious, is *Hamlet*. This is possibly due in part to the circumstance not unprecedented but still rather special that Shakespeare is here reworking a well-known, even perhaps notorious, earlier play, a circumstance which permits him to play off his own tragedy and his own protagonist against his audience's knowledge of Kyd's *Hamlet*. In any case, the self-consciousness of Shakespeare's *Hamlet* is evident. Here the play within the play is not merely a crucial element in the plot but a central figure in the theme. Here Shakespeare actually introduces a troop of professional actors to discuss their art and give us examples of their skill onstage. Here even a figure like Polonius has had some experience on the boards, acting Julius Caesar to a university audience, and nearly every character in the play from the ghost to the king is at some time or other seen metaphorically as an actor. So pervasive is the play's concern with theater that, as many critics have noted, simple terms like *show, act, play,* and *perform* seem drawn toward their specifically theatrical meaning even when they occur in neutral contexts.

If *Hamlet* is Shakespeare's most self-conscious play, the prince is surely his most self-conscious character. An actor of considerable ability himself, he is also a professed student of the drama, a scholar and critic, and a writer able on short notice to produce a speech to be inserted in a play. The prince is familiar with the stock characters of the Elizabethan stage — he lists a string of them when he hears that the players have arrived — and he is familiar, too, with at least two Elizabethan revenge plays (not counting *The Murder of Gonzago*), for at various times he burlesques both *The True Tragedy of Richard III,* that curious mixture of revenge play and chronicle history, and *The Spanish Tragedy*. Moreover, Hamlet habitually conceives of his life as a play, a drama in which he is sometimes actor and sometimes actor and playwright together. We recall immediately that in the third soliloquy ("O, what a rouge and peasant slave am I!") he speaks of having the "motive and the cue for passion" (II.ii.571). Only slightly less familiar is his description of how on the voyage to England he devised the plot of sending Rosencrantz and Guildenstern to their deaths with a forged commission:

> Being thus benetted round with villains,
> Or I could make a prologue to my brains,
> They had begun the play. I sat me down,
> Devised a new commission, wrote it fair.
> (V.ii.29–32)

And we remember that in the final scene the dying Hamlet addresses the court —

and probably the actual spectators in the Globe as well—as you "that are but mutes or audience to this act" (V.ii.336).

Hamlet's first reaction to the ghost is to leap enthusiastically into the familiar role. "Haste me" to know the truth, he cries, that I may "sweep to my revenge" (I.v.29–31). And a few lines later he launches into his vow of vengeance, the furious second soliloquy ("O all you host of heaven!") in which he calls upon heaven, earth, and hell, addresses his heart and his sinews, and pledges to wipe from his brain everything except the commandment of the ghost. It is a tissue of rhetoric passionate and hyperbolical in the true Senecan tradition, a piece of ranting of which Kyd's Hieronomo would be proud. Hamlet's self-consciousness as a revenger is suggested by the speech he requests when the players arrive, the story of Pyrrhus's bloody vengeance for his father's death. What he sees in this story is an image of his own father's fall in the crash of father Priam and, in the grief of Hecuba, the "mobled queen," an image of how Queen Gertrude ought to have behaved after her husband's death. But he also sees in Pyrrhus a horrible reflection of his own role, and, significantly, it is the prince himself who enacts the first dozen lines describing the dismal heraldry of the revenger.

Art for Hamlet is the mirror of nature, designed to provoke self-examination. Very reasonably, then, his interview with the players prompts him in the third soliloquy to consider his own motive and cue for passion, to examine how well he has performed as a revenger. Excepting his stormy vow of vengeance, Hamlet has so far controlled himself rather strictly in his duel with Claudius; he has not, by and large, indulged in much cleaving of the general ear with horrid speech in the normal manner of a revenger, and his contempt for such a manner is implicit in his description of what the common player would do with his cue: amaze the very faculties of eyes and ears and drown the stage with tears. Hamlet's aristocratic taste is for a more subtle species of drama, for plays like the one from which the story of Pyrrhus comes, which he praises to the players for being written with as much "modesty"—by which he means restraint—as cunning. Yet now, with the stock role he is to play brought home to him by the actors, Hamlet falls into the trap of judging himself by the very standards he has rejected and is disturbed by his own silence. Theatrically self-conscious as he is, Hamlet is naturally preoccupied by the relationship between playing and genuine feeling. He touches upon this in his first scene when he speaks to Gertrude of his outward "shapes of grief":

> These indeed seem,
> For they are actions that a man might play,
> But I have that within which passes show;
> These but the trappings and the suits of woe.
> (I.iii.83–86)

How is one to distinguish mere shape—in theatrical parlance the word means costume or role as well as form—from the real thing? Or conversely, if the usual shape is lacking, how can one be sure of the sutstance? After the interview with the players, it is the latter problem which concerns Hamlet, for now he wonders whether his refusal to play the revenger in the usual shape, his reluctance to drown the stage with tears, means simply that he is unpregnant of his cause. As if to prove to himself that this is not so, he winds himself up again to the ranting rhetoric of the revenger, challenging some invisible observer to call him coward, pluck his beard, tweak his nose, and finally hurling at Claudius a passionate stream of epithets:

> Bloody, bawdy villain!
> Remorseless, treacherous, lecherous, kindless villain!
> O vengeance!
>
> (II.ii.591–93)

But this time, at any rate, the role playing is conscious, and a moment later the aristocrat in Hamlet triumphs and he curses himself for a whore, a drab. To rant is cheap and vulgar; moreover, what is presently required is not the player's whorish art but action. And so, with superb irony in his choice of means, Hamlet decides to take his own kind of action:

> I'll have these players
> Play something like the murder of my father
> Before mine uncle.
>
> (II.ii.606–08)

Hamlet's difficulty is aesthetic. His problem is one of form and content, of suiting the action to the word, the word to the action—that is, of finding a satisfactory shape for his revenge. Inevitably he is drawn to the preexisting pattern of the familiar revenge plays: life imitates art. Inevitably, too, his sensibility rebels, refusing to permit him to debase himself into a ranting simpleton. I find no evidence that the idea of revenge, of taking life, is itself abhorrent to Hamlet—he is not after all a modern exponent of nonviolence—rather it is the usual style of the revenger that he disdains. He objects to passionate rhetoric because to him it typifies bestial unreason. The conventional revenger, the Hieronomo or the Titus Andronicus, responds mechanically to circumstances, beating his breast in grief and crying wildly for revenge. Such a man is Fortune's pipe, the puppet of his circumstances, and the prisoner of his own passion. When Hamlet praises the man who is not "passion's slave," he is not merely repeating a humanist commonplace; he is commenting on an immediate problem, asserting a profound objection to the role in which he has been cast. At stake, then, for Hamlet is an aesthetic principle, but it is a moral principle as well: the issue is human dignity. In a play in which earsplitting rhetoric becomes the symbol of the protagonist's burden, it is suitable that "silence" is the final word from his lips as he dies. "The rest," he says, referring to all that must be left unspoken but also to the repose of death, "is silence."

The nature of Hamlet's objection to his role is elaborated in his address to the players—a speech too frequently overlooked in interpretations of this play—which Shakespeare has included because it permits the prince to comment indirectly on his most vital concern, how one ought to play the part of a revenger. Hamlet's demand is for elegance and restraint—in a word, for dignity in playing. Lines are to be spoken "trippingly on the tongue"—that is, with grace—rather than clumsily "mouthed" in the fashion of a town crier. Nor should the player permit himself gross gestures, as sawing the air with his hand; rather he must "use all gently," and even in the very torrent, tempest, and whirlwind of passion—the moment of extremity when the temptation to strut and bellow is greatest—must "acquire and beget a temperance that may give it smoothness" (III.ii.7–8). The actor who tears a passion to tatters may win the applause of the groundlings who are only amused by noise, but he is worse than Termagant or Herod, those proverbially noisy stock characters of the old mystery plays which Hamlet disdains as ignorant and vulgar drama. It is interesting that Hamlet mentions Herod and the mythical infidel god Termagant: he means to suggest that undisciplined acting is not merely poor art, an offense against the "modesty of Nature," but an offense to all that a Christian gentleman, a humanist like himself, stands for. "O, there be players," he says a few lines later,

> that I have seen play . . . that neither having th' accent of Christians, nor the gait of Christian, pagan, nor man, have so strutted and bellowed that I have thought some of Nature's journeymen had made men, and not made them well, they imitated humanity so abominably.
>
> (III.ii.30–37)

To rage and rant is to make oneself into a monster. The crux of the issue is this: like his father—"'A was a man, take him for all in all" (I.iii.187)—Hamlet intends to be a man.

The player answers Hamlet's indictment of vulgar acting by assuring him that his company has improved its style: "I hope we have reformed that indifferently with us, sir." This complacency irritates Hamlet. "O, reform it altogether" (III.ii.39–40), he snaps in reply. Hamlet's concern is intense and personal precisely because his own life has taken the shape of a vulgar play, a crude and commonplace tragedy of revenge. The prince's response—tantalizingly like Shakespeare's, working over what must have seemed to him the crude and commonplace material of

Kyd's *Hamlet* — is to "reform it altogether." Since he cannot escape the role, Hamlet intends at least to be a revenger in a style that offends neither the modesty of nature nor his sense of human dignity. He intends to exercise discipline. I do not mean to suggest that Hamlet, like the singing gravedigger, has no feeling for his work. On the contrary, much of the drama lies in Hamlet's war with himself, his struggle to reduce his whirlwind passion to smoothness.

Hamlet and *Lear* are the only two of Shakespeare's tragedies with double plots. The Gloucester plot in *Lear* provides a relatively simple moral exemplum of one who stumbled when he saw and lost his eyes in consequence. This is a commonplace species of Elizabethan moral fable designed to set off the more complex and ambiguous story of the king. The story of Polonius's family works analogously in *Hamlet.* Each member of the family is a fairly ordinary person who serves as a foil to some aspect of Hamlet's extraordinary cunning and discipline. Polonius imagines himself a regular Machiavel, an expert at using indirections to find directions out, but compared to Hamlet he is what the prince calls him, a great baby. Ophelia, unable to control her grief, lapses into madness and a muddy death, reminding us that it is one of Hamlet's achievements that he does not go mad but only plays at insanity to disguise his true strength. And Laertes, of course, goes mad in a different fashion and becomes the model of the kind of revenger that Hamlet so disdains.

Hamlet knows he is playing a role, but Laertes is blissfully unselfconscious about his part. The prince boasts to his mother that his pulse "doth temperately keep time" (III.iv.141), but Laertes' brag is of his stereotyped rage: "That drop of blood that's calm proclaims me bastard" (IV.v.117). Laertes — to adapt Nashe's famous allusion to Kyd's old *Hamlet* — if you entreat him fair in a frosty morning, will shamelessly afford you handfuls of tragical speeches, ranting in the best manner of English Seneca:

> To hell allegiance, vows to the blackest devil,
> Conscience and grace to the profoundest pit!
> I dare damnation. To this point I stand,
> That both the worlds I give to negligence,
> Let come what comes, only I'll be revenged
> Most thoroughly for my father.
>
> (IV.v.131–36)

What comes is not quite the revenge Laertes expects, for the situation is not so simple as he supposes; rather he finds himself on account of his unthinking passion an easy instrument for Claudius to play, becoming, in his own word, the king's "organ." The advice that Polonius gave Laertes might have stood the young man in good stead if he had followed it: "Give thy thoughts no tongue, / Nor any unproportioned thought his act" (I.iii.59–60). Ironically, Polonius's words perfectly describe not Laertes' but Hamlet's approach to revenge. From the very first Hamlet has understood the practical as well as the aesthetic importance of controlling his rage. "But break my heart, for I must hold my tongue" (I.ii.159), he says at the end of the first soliloquy, and it is interesting in the light of the play's general association of lack of discipline with noise, with rant, that even here control is connected with silence.

Shakespeare contrives to have his two revengers, the typical Laertes and the extraordinary Hamlet, meet at Ophelia's grave, where the prince finds Laertes true to form tearing a passion to tatters, bellowing to be buried alive with his sister. Hamlet steps forward and the technical rhetorical terms he uses, *emphasis* and *phrase,* together with the theatrical simile of making the stars stand like "wonder-wounded hearers," like an audience, reveal his critical attitude, his professional interest in the quality of Laertes' performance:

> What is he whose grief
> Bears such an emphasis, whose phrase of sorrow
> Conjures the wand'ring stars, and makes them stand
> Like wonder-wounded hearers?
>
> (V.i.256–59)

According to the probably authentic stage direction of the first quarto, Hamlet at this point leaps into the grave alongside Laertes, suiting outrageous word to outrageous action by challenging the young man to a contest of noise, of rant. What will Laertes do to prove his love for Ophelia, weep, tear himself, drink vinegar, eat a crocodile? Hamlet will match him. Does Laertes mean to whine, to prate of being buried under a mountain higher than Pelion? Why, then Hamlet will say he'll be buried too, and let the imaginary mountain be so high that it touches the sphere of fire and makes Ossa by comparison a wart. "Nay, an thou'lt mouth," the prince says, using the same word with which he had earlier described the manner of vulgar actors, "I'll rant as well as thou" (V.i.285–86).

Hamlet is mocking Laertes' style, but the bitterness of his mockery, the nastiness of it, derives from his own sincere grief for Ophelia. In a world of overblown rhetoric, of grotesque elephantine shows, how can a man of taste and discernment be understood? Moreover, since the usual sound and fury so often signify nothing, how will a man of genuine feeling be believed? This burlesque of Laertes is Hamlet's last act of bitter rebellion against the vulgarity of his world and the role he has been constrained to play in it. Moreover, it is a reversion to his earlier and fiercer mood, the proud, contemptuous spirit of the prince before the sea voyage; for, as most critics observe, the prince who returns from sea is a changed man, resigned, detached, perhaps "tragically illuminated." Having refused to kill the king when the time was every way propitious—that is, when he found Claudius kneeling in empty not genuine prayer—and then, having chosen his own moment to act only to find that instead of the king he has murdered Polonius, Hamlet seems to have allowed his sinews to relax. He has let himself be thrust aboard ship, let himself in effect be cast onto the sea of fortune that is so common an image in Shakespeare and the Elizabethan poets, an image recalling that "sea of troubles" against which he had earlier taken arms. When the opportunity to escape the king's trap arises, Hamlet seizes it, leaping aboard the pirate ship, but what he is doing now is reacting to circumstances rather than trying to dominate them wholly. The prince returns to Denmark at once sad and amused, but, except for the single flash of "towering passion" at Ophelia's grave, relatively impassive. He has ceased to insist that he must be above being played upon by any power.

And yet, before Hamlet consents to the duel with Laertes, about which he has justified misgivings, he plays a scene with that impossible fop, Osric, the emblem of the empty courtesy of Claudius's court. Just as Hamlet earlier led Polonius through the game of cloud shapes, so now he toys with Osric, leading him to proclaim first that the weather is warm, then that it is cold, and finally warm again. At the penultimate moment, Hamlet is demonstrating that if he wished he might still play upon the king and his instruments like so many pipes. Hamlet's mocking Osric, like the scene with Laertes in the grave, recalls the early proud manner of the prince; nevertheless, Hamlet no longer seems to be in rebellion: rather than bitter contempt he displays amusement that at the end he should be forced to share the stage with a waterfly. The prince's motto is no longer "heart, lose not thy nature," but "let be." He has ceased to struggle for absolute freedom in his role, ceased to insist that he alone must be the artist who, in all senses of the term, shapes his life. He understands now that, in Laertes' words, he cannot carve for himself. One can at best be a collaborator in one's life, for there is always another artist to be taken into account, "a divinity that shapes our ends, / Rough-hew them how we will."

The Hamlet who speaks of special providence in the fall of a sparrow is not perhaps so exciting a figure as the earlier Hamlet heroically refusing to be manipulated. There is something almost superhuman in the discipline, consciousness, and cunning of the earlier Hamlet: certainly he makes superhuman demands upon himself, insisting that he be in action like an angel, in apprehension like a god. But Hamlet has discovered that, finally, he is subject to his birth, that he is neither angel nor god, and, in an ironically different sense, it can now be said of him what he said of his father, "'A was a man, take him for all." King Hamlet fought his single combat in an unfallen world of law and heraldry; his son must seek to emulate him in a corrupt world of empty chivalry and poisoned foils; and yet, in its way, Hamlet's duel with Laertes is as heroic as his father's with Fortinbras, and in his own manner Hamlet proves himself worthy of the name of soldier.

"Bear Hamlet like a soldier to the stage" (V.ii.397) is the command of Fortinbras which concludes the play, a command which not only ratifies Hamlet's heroism by using the term *soldier,* but in its theatrical allusion reminds us that much of his achievement has been in the skill with which he has played his inauspicious role. If all the world is a stage and all the men and women merely players, then the reckoning of quality must be by professional standards. By these standards Hamlet has proven himself a very great actor indeed, for he has taken a vulgar role and reformed it so that it no longer offends the modesty of nature or the dignity of man. Even a man on a tether, to pick up Polonius's image again, has a certain degree of freedom. One may be cast in a vulgar role and still win distinction in the manner the role is played. Or one may be tied to the story line of a crude melodrama and still produce a *Hamlet.*

Pre-Pepysian Theatre:
A Challenged Spectacle

Francis Barker

In pursuit of the decisive reshaping of the body politic and its subjectivity that was effected in the seventeenth century and which results in the Pepysian situation, it will be necessary to trace a path back across the years of the revolution, and to read in a text of Milton's and in the pervasive publicity of the Jacobean stage, the crisis of the older polity, and the main determinants of the outcome registered in Pepys and which in essential outline we have still to endure today. The historical settlement which preceded the bourgeois order of whose inner structure Pepys' predicament is an early instance, was profoundly different from that modernity of subjection which the revolution inaugurated. Only efforts of de-historicization similar to those practised by the Pepysian commentators, whose impressive but insidious simplicity we have [previously] noticed, could hope to achieve even a partial assimilation of the pre-revolutionary to the present.

In particular the sign of the literary greatness of Shakespeare has played a major part in remaking the late feudal world in the image of the bourgeois settlement that grew up inside it, and eventually brought it down. If not the invariability of a quotidian discourse like that of the clerk, at least its more elevated version, the timelessness of great art, has had to be mobilized in order to secure the necessary abolition of historical difference: Shakespeare's texts, their universality, their "broad humanism" — even their beauty — have served, in the hands of left and right, to secure in an alien history a value and a point of reference by which the other can be identified as the same, and thus tamed, explained, and even appreciated.

From *The Tremulous Private Body: Essays on Subjection.* © 1984 by Francis Barker. Methuen & Co., 1984. Originally entitled "A Challenged Spectacle."

This is not the place for an extensive critique of Shakespearean criticism or of the role of "Shakespeare" in British culture, but the mere citation of the commanding position of the Shakespearean text within the reception of the pre-revolutionary discursivity will suffice to identify the order of difficulty to be encountered in trying to insist on the necessity of redrawing the map of that other world. In one sense, of course, all history is contemporary history, so what is at issue is not that Shakespeare's corpus has been reproduced in order to be reshaped to present needs: this is the general task of all historiography, and to believe otherwise would be to advance a hubristic objectivism. Nor is it necessary to deny that there are features in the Shakespearean text which lend themselves particularly well to the uses that have been found for them: this probably accounts for their "greatness" in so far as the literary tradition has been able to celebrate what is, unknown to itself, a narcissistic self-confirmation, "recognizing" in Shakespeare's transitional and contradictory *oeuvre* those elements which are truly its own. It is simply that another history must be written if our account of that corporal past is not to be merely a case of recapitulating in the pre-revolutionary texts the themes and structures which it was precisely the task of the revolution to establish, by *destroying* the polity whose complex index the Shakespearean discourse was.

The effort of historiographical denial of the situation for discourse and the body *abolished* by the Pepysian settlement is stamped on the other side of the coin of Shakespeare's present greatness: the minority of the other Jacobeans. Above all it is evident in the indictment for sensationalism which has so frequently secured the Jacobeans' inferior status in the calm and hygienic moral order that obtains in literary criticism, if nowhere else. In part, the charge of sensationalism goes to the substantive and recklessly bodily contents of the scenes and images that are said to elicit the sensation, and we shall return to them; but also, connected inextricably with this, it more covertly denigrates the Jacobean *mode* of representation itself, which is also alien to the history which succeeded it and the historiography which has refused its significance. The reception of the Jacobean text has proceeded in a fashion entirely subjugated to the partitive sign of the *literary* greatness of Shakespeare's verse: the word has found a place of privilege over the image. It is against this measure that a crux like that in which the Duchess of Malfi is shown the wax figures of the corpses—the bodies—of Antonio and his children by her tormentors, which is in essence spectacular although words are also spoken, has been judged in principle inferior to the kind so frequent in Shakespeare which is effected, allegedly, in language although accompanied by stage business. But what is at stake in opposing this organizing principle of the traditional reproduction of the Jacobean representational situation is not the banal plea for the "living theatre" against the academicism of the play-*text;* still less is it designed to reinforce an existentially untenable opposition between word and image, and thus to enforce a spurious choice between them, but rather an assessment of the cost of this organization of the reception, recognizing the subsequent decisions that have been made regarding the relative weighting of language and spectacle within the historical retroaction of developments familiar to Pepys and his epoch, but not yet fulfilled in the theatre-world of the early seventeenth century.

Those who have attacked sensationalism would doubtless deny that they are carrying out the belated cultural work of the bourgeois revolution: but it is hard not to see in the attack on sensation the hand of a Protestant asceticism, and in the demotion of the spectacle a continuity with the seventeenth century's own iconoclasm in favour of the Word. But then history has a way of working itself out behind the backs of its actors, as Marx pointed out. The potential for depravity of the moral sensibilities in the exercise of visual representation was an argument familiar to the period, and one repeatedly mobilized at the time against the liberty and the insistence of the visual in the Jacobean world theatre. It is thus not *necessary* to assume that a lack of goodwill, nor even an ignorant prejudice has governed the hierarchization of Shakespeare and "the others." Although it is true that the politics of a Middleton are more unacceptably radical, and that the reconciliatory complacency attempted by reaches of Shakespeare's discourse finds its critical opposite in the troubled, mordant sensibility of a Webster or a Tourneur, it is the more historical, and so more deeply political, rejection of the visibility of the mode of representation that controls the evaluations of the Jacobean texts as we receive them.

At the level of representation what has been elided — or acknowledged only in the condemnatory form of the charge of sensationalism — is the theatricality of this theatre, the innocent foregrounding of its device.

When a play like *The Revenger's Tragedy* cannot be regarded as particularly extraordinary for the fact that, almost without content and verging constantly on self-parody, it moves from one quoted stage device to another, we are clearly far from that occlusion of writing itself which is effected in the post-Pepysian world by the attribution to discourse of an instrumental transparency. Tourneur's text is constructed by tireless reference to its own signifying; each sequence is a matrix of citation, imitation and reworking of the range of theatrical tropes and mechanisms at work on the Jacobean stage, and in this sense is only a usefully typical example of the early seventeenth-century theatre as a whole. The masques and the masks, the quaint devices and the stereotyping of character and situation, the relentless artifice and even the all-pervasive metaphor of the theatre itself are not the exceptions to the rule of this theatre, but the rule itself. Even Shakespeare's writing culminates in *The Tempest,* that spectacle which has been criticized so frequently for its improbability, its lack of narrative, its absence of dramatic tension, criticized, in short, for being what the formalists would have called "unmotivated."

But if the Jacobean texts continually remark beneath their breath or in loud clear voices, "Regard me: I am a play," or if it was sometimes necessary for them, in order to achieve a sufficient extraordinariness, to double the stakes and let the play within the play raise the density of representation to the second power, they are not thus unacceptable to naturalizing criticism on aesthetic grounds alone, but because they share an unbroken continuity—across the proscenium *which is not there*—with the world in which they were performed, and which they perform. It is difficult, perhaps impossible, now to imagine a settlement in which the means of representation are so clearly visible as such: an artisanal world in which the device is naked not out of polemical technique but as its normal condition; a discursive situation before production has quite "disappeared" into, in one of its modalities, the closed factory, or at the level of representation, into the conventions of that bourgeois naturalism which has nothing to do with nature, and everything to do with naturalizing the suppression of the signs of the artefact's production. A world of other visibilities than our own, which is founded on *their* elision, and whose suppression the reception of the texts rehearses.

Brecht understood this when he turned back to this early stage for material for his own alienated political theatre. But if Brecht's project was, by the elaboration of that series of theatrical interventions now known by the portmanteau "alienation effect," to distance and break the mystificatory illusion near the end of its reign, the Jacobean theatre was, so to speak, anti-naturalist before the event. If there are seeds of an incipient naturalism growing up within it, so are there instances of its struggling to contain and ward them off: if Hamlet called on discourse to hold a mirror up to nature, at least the mirror could be seen for what it was. And nowhere more so—in a fine example of the typical lying at what we had been told were the margins—than in a text that criticism has consigned to obscurity, but which was in its time the most notorious of political plays; suppressed by troops after an unprecedented nine consecutive performances but none the less containing the essential figure of this unacceptable visuality where representation is itself present to representation. In the second seduction scene of Thomas Middleton's *A Game at Chesse* (the "characters" and the general figuration of the play are worked out within a flagrantly unnatural chess trope) the White Queen's Pawn is momentarily entrapped by the device of an Egyptian mirror. She has been told that it is an enchanted mirror which will show her the man she is to marry. She is the desired object of the Black Bishop's Pawn, a Jesuit, who has attempted her seduction once by giving her a tract on religious obedience and, after the chaste White Queen's Pawn has absorbed its lesson, exacting a kiss as an exercise in subordination to a spiritual superior. Now, in the second attempt, the Black Jesuit appears on stage behind the White Queen's Pawn disguised as a gallant "in rich attire like an apparition." She, catching sight of what she thinks is a magic and privileged perception but which, even in the reality of the play, is no more than a plain glass, is thus captivated by his image. In the scene immediately following the Jesuit encounters the Black Knight's Pawn, a castrator, who at once recognizes the still-disguised priest by deciphering the coded inscription on his hatband (undercover Jesuit missionaries used such devices for mutual recognition).

The spectacular layers of this scene are complex. The woman is not allowed to look on reality direct but must glimpse it in a mirror which offers extraordinary sight but which is in fact a plain source of danger. The reality is itself disguised. In contrast to the White Queen's Pawn's earlier act of inefficient reading by which she became ensnared in power and vulnerable to sexual assault by having interpreted written signs literally and naïvely, the Black Knight's Pawn is able to read successfully through the dissembled text. And the devices are laid bare as the play, in its radicalism, uncertainizes its own ideological categories by drawing attention to their constructedness by means of the arbitrary and unconcealed theatricality with which it must engineer the White, Protestant, English, virtuous Pawn's escape from Black, Catholic, Spanish perfidy. To do this it first uses the cover of an unmotivated "noise within," and it then extricates her from threatening specular captation by the equally unmotivated eventuality of another, Black, character's stratagems, which are not intrinsically related to the matter in hand but which unconsciously give political viability to the "wrong" side. But of overriding and exemplary importance for this theatre is the fact that the whole is itself surrounded by another set of lines of sight by which the audience views everything without illusion. It is always aware of the real nature of the dissimulated glass, the "identity" behind the disguise, and the functional purpose of the episode as a whole, although these are hidden from the White Pawn. There *is* a visual obscurity here, but it is confined to the stage, and there, to the object pawn against whose body the seduction and the assault are directed. It is not a deep obscurity in the sense that the place from which the scene is viewed is either clouded or confused.

The decoding of this structure involves a significant account of the gendering of the instance of power, to which we shall return [elsewhere], linked to a historical transition from sight to script as the medium of political facility and encratic difficulty: that the efficient reader is also a male castrator no doubt recounts a corporeal history of its own. But above all it is necessary to see that the problematicity of the scene — its gender dominations and its ideological and, indeed, political transaction — are realized in the graphic stage devices which overwhelmingly mark the visual and the specular as the plane of this theatre's signification.

Only beyond our own naturalism will it be possible fully to comprehend that the audience was never captivated by the illusion because the spectacle never produced itself as other than what it was. This is why it is right to speak of the Jacobean device as innocent (from a representational rather than from a moral or political point of view): the device did not need to be at a distance when its erasure had not yet been secured. A subsequent cultural and historical movement clawed representation back from these outer limits of visibility into the duller and more treacherous reaches where the signifier is effaced and the specific gravity of representation bled off in favour of the theoretically naïve but politically powerful regime of the simple transcription of nature itself. The bourgeoisie, forgetting its revolutionary past as quickly as was decently possible (and, in England at least, before the classes beneath could learn anything of significance from it), soon constructs its own discursivity within which it is next to impossible to think the proposition that the represented—historical reality itself—is a thing produced, and not as in Pepys, voyeuristically and largely passively contemplated. It remains a pressing contemporary task to continue Brecht's work and in transvaluating the reception of the pre-naturalist Jacobean theatre to mobilize it as a critical weapon against the very naturalism that stifled it: not complacently to elide its difference, but to redeem, in a sense which Benjamin would have understood, that alterity.

But the reception of the Jacobean text-world we have been discussing does not reject solely these formal properties of that discursivity. It is their inextricable conjunction with the corporeality of the early seventeenth-century world that fully explains their denial by criticism anxious to disavow a materiality on whose de-realization its tradition is founded. Almost without exception, the depravity of the tragic dramatist who resorts to sensation is most clearly in evidence, it is said, in the presentation on stage of the body and the violence done to it. But is it utterly accidental, or even simply Webster's doubtful opportunism, that in the waxworks scene in *The Duchess of Malfi* it is the *corpses* of Antonio and the children that are displayed; or that in the same series of torments, at the far limits of theatrical pathos, the masque of the lunatics, doubling the spectacle within the spectacle, is in such close proximity to the episode of the severed hand? Is there not, perhaps, a more internally robust connection between the dramatic scene and the seen body than one merely of perversity of taste when Macbeth's head is brought in, or Annabella's bleeding heart on the point of a dagger? Or when the body of Sejanus, like that of Cinna the poet before him, is torn in pieces at a moment of politics in a mass form? It is, of course, possible that merely a certain delicacy of touch in respect of corporeal pain, an artistry which we have lost, smears the poison of Vindice's revenge on the lipless skull of his raped and murdered mistress, from where, transmitted by a half-dead kiss, it eats away first the mouth and then the brain of the old Duke, while Hippolito holds down the man's dying tongue with the point of his knife. Or perhaps just a reflection of the available technology? But it would be better, more historically sensitive, to ask what inner cast of sociality governs the putting out of Gloucester's eyes and the corporeal extravagance of the now significantly seldom performed *Titus Andronicus*. For despite the fact that our own world has its share of torturers, a mark of difference from ourselves can be read in these and the other versions of the spectacular body with which the Jacobean stage is redolent. Especially when beyond that missing proscenium, in "reality" itself, lies the mutilation that Prynne suffered for his discursive offences, or the public death which was exacted on another stage (Marvell does not fail to grasp the essential connection in his "An Horatian ode") of the king himself. These images of the body are not instances of the arbitrary perversity of single dramatists, nor even the casual brutalities hidden away in underground cells or distant camps by violent but irredeemably furtive governments, but the insistence in the spectacle of a corporeality which is quite other than our own. The visibility of this body in pain—the pre-disciplinary body extant before that incarceration which is disclosed, in their different ways, both by Foucault's work and by the Pepysian text—is systemic rather than personal; not the issue of an aberrant exhibitionism, but formed across the whole surface of the social as the locus of the desire, the revenge, the power and the misery of this world.

The spectacular body in whose language Lady Macbeth must define her conditions and demands, and against whose measure Hamlet's anachronistic inwardness will have to be assessed, is everywhere present as the object and site of the confrontations which articulate the drama of this settlement. Continually evoked and displayed, close to language itself, the impersonal body is almost promiscuous in the repeated urgency with which it installs itself in the metaphors and concepts of this world, as well as in its practical situations. But properly it can only be regarded in this way because a certain emphasis is polemically necessary against the decentration in later suffers in history and in historiography alike. "That a king may go a progress through the guts of a beggar" (*Hamlet*, IV.iii.29–30) is extraordinary (if it is so at all) for its insistence of the democracy of mortality in contrast with the hierarchized body politic of the living world, not for the corporeal expression in which the idea emerges. The proliferation in the dramatic, philosophical and political texts of the period of corporeal images which have become dead metaphors for us—by a structured forgetting rather than by innocent historical wastage—are the indices of a social order in which the body has a central and irreducible place. Whether judicially tortured as the visible sign of the vengeance of the king on the transgressor, or disassembled lovingly on stage in the cause of poetry, it is the crucial fulcrum and crossing point of the lines of force, discursive and physical, which form this world as the place of danger and aspiration to which the

Jacobean texts repeatedly attest. The glorious cruelties of the Jacobean theatre thus articulate a mode of corporeality which is structural to its world. Although the involvement of the body in punishment is only an essential and typical section across the way in which discourse invests it with a fundamental (and therefore, in this world, *superficial*) meaning, it none the less represents a generalized condition under which the body, living or dead, is not that effaced residue which it is to become, beneath or behind the proper realm of discourse, but a materiality that is fully and unashamedly involved in the processes of domination and resistance which are the inner substance of social life. The stage of representation and that other scaffold of corporal punishment are, as Marvell saw, effectively continuous with each other. On both, the spectacularly visible body is fully in place within signification, coterminous with the plane of representation itself.

Unlike the secret half-life to which the Pepysian corporeality has been assigned, but from which it continues nevertheless to agitate the newly sovereign speech of a disembodied and Cartesian subjectivity, this early body lies athwart that divide between subject and object, discourse and world, that characterizes the later dispensation. The body of the world and that of the text are frequently identified with each other in the ideology of the Renaissance, but the metaphor should be understood with a nominalism appropriate to a period that antedates the deleterious separations on which modernity is founded. At the signifying centre of the culture they are at one with each other in the figure of the Passion, where the word and the body are inextricably identified in an act of punishment and signification from which all other meanings flow: the spirit who is the one real Subject of this world is wholly immanent, incarnate, in the flesh. The Jacobean body is at once sacred and profane, tortured and celebrated in the same gesture, because it traverses even the polarities of the culture's investments: or rather, it is the medium and the substance in which, ultimately, those meanings are inscribed. It has this polyvalent but unambiguous status because drawn on its surface are the means by which the culture, even at its most metaphysical, can determine not only its consonances but its inner discords as well. The underpinnings of the more quotidian disputes which texture the life of this society return in their grounding to that unseparated word made flesh which is the principle of its representational practices (practices which cannot, thus, be regarded as *representational* in the strictest sense). A mode of discourse operates here which, basing itself in incarnation, exercises a unitary *presence* of meaning of which the spectacular body is both the symbol and the instance.

That the body we see is so frequently presented in fragments, or in the process of its effective dismemberment, no doubt indicates that contradiction is already growing up within this system of presence, and that the deadly subjectivity of the modern is already beginning to emerge and to round vindictively on the most prevalent emblem of the discursive order it supersedes. But despite the violence unleashed against the body, it has not yet been quenched. However much it has been subsequently ignored, it remains in the texts themselves as a vital, full materiality. The Jacobean body—the object, certainly, of terrible pressures—is distributed irreducibly throughout a theatre whose political and cultural centrality can only be measured against the marginality of the theatre today; and beyond the theatre it exists in a world whose most subtle inner organization is so different from that of our own not least because of the part played by this body in it. In the fullest sense which it is now possible to conceive, from the other side of our own carnal guilt, it is a *corporeal* body, which, if it is already touched by the metaphysic of its later erasure, still contains a charge which, set off by the violent hands laid on it, will illuminate the scene, incite difference, and ignite poetry. This spectacular visible body is the proper gauge of what the bourgeoisie has had to forget.

It is also therefore the body proper to that bright plenum which surrounds, but fails initially to include, Hamlet, whose world is laden, top-heavy with visibility: a world where everyone, in principle at least, assisted at the spectacle. In the crowded chamber soldiers lean on their halberds, perhaps half-listening, or just waiting for the changing of the guard. Knots of courtiers are gathered beneath the dais, absorbing the king's words: some, like Osric, fawning: others no doubt harbouring their own reservations about the legitimacy of the succession but, experienced in the naked, sudden and direct forms of power which mark their epoch, gravely keeping their own counsel. Servants move among the throng with sweet wine and honey cakes. Court officials are busy at a side-table near the throne. One cuts a quill with a small silver penknife, while another turns the ambassadors' letters patent in his delicate white fingers. Rumours of war stir and eddy there. The queen's face is expressionless, mask-like. A musician tunes a string in the alcove beside the great fireplace, crouched over his lute, one ankle resting on the other knee, the instrument cradled against his leg. Two hunting dogs lie sleepily on the rushes while the business of state murmurs around them. The sombre prince waits to one side.

There is apparently nothing here that cannot be seen. From the first apparition to that last procession when four sad captains carry the dead prince to the stage where his body will lie displayed *in state,* the moment of reality is the moment of sight. Elsinore is a place of spies and actors, actual and metaphorical, where scenes are played out to acknowledged and unacknowledged audiences, and where sight transfixes or is stolen, but is never doubted as the dominant mode of a (sometimes fraudulent) access.

The *teatrum mundi* has been taken as a metaphor, and this is today an intelligible mistake. But it is closer to a literalism in respect of this social plenum than a metaphor of contingent artifice. There is no well-founded division between those who perform and those who are spectators, between the subjects and objects of communicative sight: as one performs before another, she or he is at once regarded by a third, and so on throughout a network of asymmetrical observations patterning the entire space of being. It is not that there are no professional actors in this world (although they are of comparatively recent emergence, and their historical moment is properly yet to come), but that their condition repeats so closely—as the Jacobean texts continually insist—that of those others who are, of necessity here, but poor players of life itself. A condition, moreover, in which the *exteriority* of meaning is enacted in the foregrounding of the role and the part which the theatrical figuration of this world deploys. In *Hamlet,* social life is a succession of brightly lit tableaux set against black backgrounds whose darkness is not the symbol of a mysterious alterity, but simply the meaninglessness of the void beyond the surface of signification itself.

The spectacle is not without its ambiguities, however, for in Denmark one may smile and smile and be a villain. Nor does the visual fullness of Hamlet's world entail the assumption of a plenitude of utter transparency: we must always beware the myth of better times that lies in wait for all our projections back beyond the modern. But it simply affirms that the dominant of this world, and of these texts, crossed and recrossed by dense lines of sight, is its spectacularity functioning as a concrete metaphor of presence; that even the error of this world is a riddle in its crowded visuality. So many of the notorious cruces for interpretative criticism and for the figures that populate this world turn upon ambiguous or deceitful appearance, that the commonplace name of seeming has been given to the problem. It is less frequently remarked that its system of signification is still secure enough, even as the crisis gathers in *Hamlet,* for false appearances only to be discernible as such against the surer measure of the true and the real, whether this be personified on stage in an omniscient dramaturge-seer, a Prospero, or vouchsafed to a knowing audience which accepts by convention that it can penetrate the disguise, while those within the action cannot. But in either case, and even if seeming is not the *profound* difficulty which criticism in its paucity has tried to make it, the arena of error and danger, of truth and its dissimulation, remains this complex of signs, devices and visualities.

Hamlet's world is riddled with difficulties: its alienation on the other side of naturalism, its own internal seeming, and, as we shall see, an incipient modernity. But in achieving its most explicit character in an interplay of visibilities, is this world not also one of relentless surfaces, without depth or mystery? This question formulates a crucial problem. For the moment it can be answered provisionally if enigmatically by remarking that it has only one modern depth because only one individual inhabits it, and even he is putative. For now it is enough to define the kind of obscurity, of difficulty, that is truly this world's and not his. Although the play, by turns ghostly and conspiratorial, is not lacking in the promise of mystery, it is of a very qualified kind, for all the conspiracies of the night are revealed, finally, and the whispered conversations overheard. There is little that remains ultimately opaque. Even Ophelia's madness moves in this world as the emblem of an indelible grief, but not as a diagnostic problem. Its typical figure is not Hamlet, but Polonius behind the arras. A thin veil hangs between him and the action that destroys him, a tapestry that conceals his presence but does not transform it. He learns nothing there. He dies because he is hidden, but his slaughter is one of the casual ones which Horatio survives to narrate in a place conservatively simplified again by Hamlet's *necessary* death. In no essential way do Polonius and his destiny encounter each other in the passage of the prince's blade through the fibres of the arras; his mistake, if such it is, is to be momentarily out of sight, not to be worthy or even desirous of such a death.

This world achieves its depth not in the figure of interiority by which the concealed inside is of another quality from what is external, but by a *doubling of the surface*. Just as *The Mousetrap* layers a spectacle within the spectacle, so the sheet of the action may be folded over until an unexpected contact is made and a sudden discharge of violence touched off. But the meaning of the action is generated in the productivity of the figures inscribed on the planer surfaces of the body of the text. *The Mousetrap* does not function to discover a truth (except in the most literal sense of discovery), for this is one of the few murder stories where the identity of the killer is revealed on the first page—and even if ghosts cannot be trusted, this operates as a vehicle of Hamlet's delay rather than as a real epistemological problem—but serves to organize in transit the necessary anxiety which must flow from and around the incestuous usurpation. It acts as a bridge between nodes of the extremely attenuated action (not much actually happens at Elsinore) rather than as an instrument of the revelation of a hidden mystery. This accounts for its curious, frustrated lack of consequence. Hamlet does not sweep to his revenge impelled by the proof of Claudius's guilt which the play within the play provides, because it isn't a *proof* of anything that was in doubt. *The Mousetrap* draws a line across the surface, an articulation in the diagram of the action. It functions to extend time rather than to excavate a hidden level of reality. Apart from the one great exception to the rule of this theatre's space, the reality of this world is utterly single, however it may be folded over on itself.

That Hamlet's first argument with his stepfather takes place in the crowded council chamber marks off this spectacular, corporeal sovereignty from the polity which is to succeed it. There is, however, no difficulty in recognizing, even from the present, the scene of the state. The language and the costume may not be that of our own day, but nor are we—on the surface—without sure points of reference here. Conducted under a different historical form, but clearly identifiable as such even from the contemporary standpoint of a very different experience of the political, central affairs of state are centrally enacted: the succession of rule, and the emergency of war. Claudius's opening disquisition on the haste with which his marriage to Gertrude has followed on the death of the former king her husband, by way of a nicely turned contrast between mourning and celebration, manages to sound at once sorrowing and festive. It is the accomplished palliative speech of an adept politician reassuring anxieties at home. He is convincing, genial, magnanimous, clearly adroit in managing councils of state. The next item of business touches foreign policy: Fortinbras has sharked up his list of lawless resolutes in the marches and now challenges for the control of disputed territory. Old rights are involved, not least the honour of the dead king, which Claudius does not fail to mention, skilfully linking the external threat to the internal problem, subtly buttressing his legitimacy by establishing himself as a defender of the memory of his predecessor against the foreign invader. War grows out of such things, and Denmark's armourers and shipwrights are already preparing for the conflict, but Claudius will pursue the options of diplomacy before unleashing the violence of this warlike state against the mercenaries. A certain political circumspection governs his instructions to the ambassadors, who are fiercely ordered not to overstep the limits of their commission. In this, the primal scene of the play, the fully political concerns of the internal and external security of the realm itself are dramatized. Written at a moment in England's political history when both press heavily on the real kingdom, the scene delineates process of government with a clarity that is as economical as it is essential. The destiny of an entire society is gathered into these few lines and placed before audiences who will themselves participate at a drama of historical crisis. Denmark and England each stand on a threshold of change: by the end a certain greatness will have gone out of one; revolution will transform the other.

But there is an anachronistic temptation to read back from the present and identify, in the next business of the scene, as it shifts from the empowering of the ambassadors to the matter of Laertes's departure from court, with a *caesura* dividing off the political state from the more intimate textures of family life. Hardly high policy on a level with what has already been transacted in this busy hall, does this episode not serve to reformulate the scene, and to manage a transition from the public space to the personal and domestic argument with Hamlet that is to follow? To think so would be to commit a signal historical mistake. At most the items on this agenda are organized according to a descending order of importance, and even that is questionable in view of the subsequent unfolding of the action. The narrative of the drama (which should not, in any event, be confused with the form of the social situation it discloses) will foreground the particular trajectories of Hamlet substantially, and Laertes to an extent; but this must not be allowed to occlude its location of these destinies within the menace of the wider crisis, and more profoundly, within a density and order of being that defers the modern division.

In sharp contrast to the separations which the Pepysian text describes, in this polity, Laertes's departure is fully *in place* in the business of state. The king's permission — sued for in full council — doubles, complements, sanctions and completes the reluctant permission of the biological father. The scene inscribes within itself not a separation of spheres but that relation of subordinate correspondence, theorized with varying degrees of mysticism at the time, between the father who is as a king in the family and the king who is as a father in the state. Nor should this similitude be thought as pallid analogy or distant likeness. It is stricter than homology, and constitutes an essential link in a chain of ideal connections that ground sociality itself in a theory of kingship and kinship which was practised in an array of political, juridicial and cultural institutions, and which articulates a social body that is layered, figured, but one. Organized under the general form of hierarchy, sanctioned in practice by force and metaphysically by God the King and God the Father whose just order it reflects, the single realm describes a full place, tense with patterns of fealty, reciprocity, obligation and command. The figure of the king guarantees, as locus and source of power and as master-signifier, a network of subsidiary relations which constitute the real practice and intelligibility of the lives of subjects.

If the body of the Passion is the foundation of this world's signifying, at the same time the body of the king is its coherent temporal instance, the body that encompasses all mundane bodies within its build. But the subjection at work here is not that modern form for which the ambitiously inappropriate name of "consciousness" is frequently used. Pre-bourgeois subjection does not properly involve subjectivity at all, but a condition of dependent membership in which place and articulation are defined not by an interiorized self-recognition — complete or partial, percipient or unknowing, efficient or rebellious — (of none the less socially constituted subject-positions), but by incorporation in the body politic which is the king's body in its social form. With a clarity now hard to recapture, the social plenum *is* the body of the king, and membership of this anatomy is the deep structural form of all being in the secular realm. Where post-Pepysian subjection will distance the external world in order to construct subjectivity as the (imaginary) property of inner selfhood, this sovereignty achieves its domination by other means, across an articulated but single ground. It establishes a constitution within which subjects are profoundly implicated not because they "know their place" (as in the modern form when it is effective) but because alterity of placement is always already encoded as unthinkable. Or at least no more conceivable than the absurd proposition that the arm could take the place of the spleen. This did not prevent rebellion, but the heavy price legitimacy extracts for such an act is the burden of dismembering the frame of place and sense itself.

In this scene, in *Hamlet,* the king and the biological father happen to be different people. But not far away in the *oeuvre,* in a significantly more conservative text, they are identical. When Lear sets his tragic action in motion by dividing the indivisible kingdom, there are a number of different registers to his error (one of the glories of the Renaissance is the pre-Rationalist *complexity* of its error). The historical register involves regression across a century of painful development. Under the Tudor dynasty England had emerged from internal wars to lay the groundwork of a nation state. The Crown, in breaking the authority of the feudal magnates and in rearticulating under its own sovereignty that of the Church, acquired the national monopoly of the means of both persuasion and violence. By skilful manipulation of class and factional alliances both with and over the heads of the lords ecclesiastical and temporal, it reorganized the power previously vested in them. The imposition of a professional central bureaucracy, and of local administrative and judicial government staffed increasingly by royal appointees, appeared to disseminate control at the same time as it effectively gathered it to the writ of the Crown. But Lear, in his *historical* folly, refragments the realm by dividing it among his daughters and re-establishing, under a nominal and ineffectual monarch, powerful and competitive baronial factions, whose gender only serves to underline their monstrous character.

If today an effort of retrospective imagination is needed in order to perceive the catastrophic enormity of this, to contemporaries its implications were plain and fearsome. And not simply because of the threat posed by this dismemberment of the integrity of the realm. For in another register, but at the identical moment and not as a consequential effect, Lear's action—which is already close to that madness that will soon bear down on him—also disarticulates the order of the family. If Hamlet's first argument with Claudius takes place in state, in the first scene of *Lear* the fusion (of what is in any case not yet separate) is also total. Even without that signal blindness which permeates the play as a terrible instance of debility in the spectacular kingdom and whose first act is to misrecognize Cordelia and cast her, rather than her sisters, in the role of rebellious daughter-subject, the king's original intention of a tripartite division of the realm and the family violates an essential coherence between them both. Its intention threatens to disassemble authority relations fundamental to this patriarchal sovereignty, and to the very code of being it describes. Lear cannot abdicate his position, in family or state, as if it were the public office of a later polity. In this settlement, soon to be unsettled and surrendered to lawlessness because the place of the king-father from which the law is uttered is soon to be emptied, subjects are located in places not by the *apparently* auxiliary contingency of the later constitution, but by an essential fit, by necessary bonds of nature articulating the political anatomy of the king's body. Although disorder in the family, in the state and in the faculties of the soul—and, indeed, in cosmic nature—can act as metaphors for each other, their substantial interrelation is more profound than poetic artifice: they are all grounded at once in the same inner correspondence whose transgression risks the disarticulation of reality itself. It is with the *same* gesture of division that Lear fissures his kingdom, his family and his reason, for on this scene the state, kinship and sense repeat and extend into each other without break.

Thus Laertes's suit for permission to travel and the fourth item on the agenda which is much more problematic from the standpoint of the present—Hamlet's melancholic excess of mourning, and the Oedipal drama that begins to speak itself there—are heard in the crowded council chamber. What would appear under the new regime as private matters exist in an as yet undivided continuum with the succession and the gathering war. The public and the private as strong, mutually defining, mutually exclusive categories, each describing separate terrains with distinct contents, practices and discourses, are not yet extant. In *Hamlet* and in *Lear*, and in the wider sovereignty they disclose, the space of being, the society, the world—what you will—is ordered along different lines from those that fissure our own situation. This is not to insist that there is no aloneness there. Ophelia's lonely epithet for Hamlet himself—"The glass of fashion and the mould of form, / The observ'd of all observers" (IV.i.156–57)—certainly marks out around the prince, in significantly specular language, a penumbra of solitude. But this is not a private condition. The keynote is the very visibility with which the space is delineated: it is the pertinent metaphor, as concrete as any could be, for the indivisibility of the plenum. The sovereignty that governs this space—however insecure it is growing as it registers in the resort to the figure of the spy, or in Lear's and Gloucester's blindness, its progressive *failure to see*—is represented by the all-pervading access which the spectacle provides. This is why so many stand around, paying attention or not, near the action at the throne, in the centre of the kingdom and of the family. They and we are attentive or indifferent, but *necessary* spectators here, not because the action only acquires its meaning when it is apprehended by an audience for whom it is played out, but because no other conditions are extant. In the same way as what is seen does not take place in public, so what is not seen by all does not work itself out in private. What is secret in this world—the conspiracies of the night, two figures who stand together on an empty beach—does not correspond to that modern condition of privacy in which the Pepysian subject is incarcerated. Here even solitude, while it may be a form of torture, is a figure of the whole, contingent on the local and momentary situation, but not a rent in the social fabric as such.

And yet, to return to the great hall, which has been named with an aptness that is uncanny the *presence* chamber (for everything in this sovereignty is exactingly present, sanctioned by the real or in principle proximity of the body of the king), we must take the measure of the one great exception to the rule of this world: beside the throne, slightly apart from the others, his head bowed in thought, stands the Oedipal prince. In what are almost the first words we hear him speak, a claim is made for modern depth, for qualitative distinction from the corporeal order of the spectacle:

> Seems, madam! nay it is, I know not 'seems'.
> 'Tis not alone my inky cloak, good mother,
> Nor customary suits of solemn black,
> Nor windy suspiration of forced breath,
> No, nor the fruitful river in the eye,
> Nor the dejected haviour of the visage,
> Together with all forms, modes, shapes of grief,
> That can denote me truly. These indeed seem,
> For they are actions that a man might play,
> But I have that within that passes show,
> These but the trappings and the suits of woe.
>
> (I.ii.75–86)

Hamlet asserts against the devices of the world an essential interiority. If the "forms, modes, shapes" fail to denote him truly it is because in him a separation has already opened up between the inner reality of the subject, living itself, as "that within that passes show," and an inauthentic exterior: and in that opening there begins to insist, however prematurely, the figure that is to dominate and organize bourgeois culture. Seen from the viewpoint of this speech, the narrative of *Hamlet* is nothing but the prince's evasion of a series of positionalities offered to him by the social setting. From the moment when the ghost of his father lays on him the burden of vengeance, his passage through the drama is the refusal of — or, at most, the parodic and uncommitted participation in — the roles of courtier, lover, son, politician, swordsman, and so on. Even the central task of revenge provides, in its deferral, no more than a major axis of the play's duration. But in dismissing these modes, or "actions" as he calls them, Hamlet utters, against the substance of the spectacular plenum which is now reduced in his eyes to a factitious artificiality "that a man might play," a first demand for the modern subject. In the name, now, not of the reign of the body but of the secular soul, an interior subjectivity begins to speak here — an I which, if it encounters the world in anything more than a quizzical and contemplative manner, must alienate itself into an environment which inevitably traduces the richness of the subject by its mute and resistant externality. An early embarrassment for bourgeois ideology, and one of which Hamlet is in part an early victim, was that even as it had to legitimize the active appropriation of the world, it also had to encode its subject as an individual, privatized and largely passive "consciousness" systematically detached from a world which is thus beyond its grasp: for all its insistence on the world as tractable raw object it none the less constructs a subjectivity whose form is that of the unique and intransitive soul, centred in meanings which are apparently its alone.

But this interiority remains, in *Hamlet,* gestural. "The heart of my mystery" (III.ii.368–69), as he describes it to Guildenstern in another place, is the real opacity of the text. Unlike those other obscurities of seeming which are *proper* to the spectacle, the truth and density of *this* mystery can never be apprehended. The deceptions of the plenum which surrounds Hamlet are always ultimately identifiable as such, and therefore only obscure for a few or within some tactical situation of the drama as it unfolds: they are never beyond the reach of its epistemology. But Hamlet's inner mystery is not of this order. Neither those who seek it out within the play, who try to discover whether he is mad in reality or "in craft," nor the audience who overhear so many examples of the rhetorical form proper to this isolated subjectivity, the soliloquy, are ever placed by the text in a position from which it can be grasped. It perdures as a central obscurity which cannot be dramatized. The historical prematurity of this subjectivity places it outside the limits of the text-world in which it is as yet emergent only in a promissory form. The text continually offers to fulfil the claim of that first speech, but whenever it appears that the claimed core of that within which passes the show of the spectacle will be substantially articulated, Hamlet's riddling, antic language shifts its ground and the text slides away from essence into a further deferral of the mystery. But if the text cannot dramatize this subjectivity, it can at least display its impossibility, when Hamlet offers a metaphor of himself, of his self, to Guildenstern who is an instrument, purely, of the king, and signally lacking any form of interiority. Challenging Guildenstern to "pluck out the heart" of his mystery — in language sufficiently corporeal to point the failure — Hamlet gives him the recorder which he cannot play, although he would, in Hamlet's conceit, "sound" the "compass" of the prince. The hollow pipe is the refutation of the metaphysic of soul which the play signals but cannot realize. For Hamlet, in a sense doubtless unknown to him, is truly this hollow reed which will "discourse most eloquent music" but is none the less vacuous for that. At the centre of Hamlet, in the interior of his mystery, there is, in short, nothing. The promised essence remains beyond the scope of the text's signification: or rather, signals the limit of the signification of this world by marking out the site of an absence it cannot fill. It gestures towards a place for subjectivity, but both are anachronistic and belong to a historical order whose outline has so far only been sketched out.

It is into this breach in Hamlet that successive generations of criticism—especially Romantic and post-Romantic variants—have stepped in order to fill the vacuum and, in explaining Hamlet, to explain him away. This effort to dissipate the challenge he represents is partly explained by the need to remake the Jacobean settlement in the eternal image of the bourgeois world, and partly by a more subversive potential in the prince. Accounts of his unresolved Oedipus complex, his paranoia—both clinical and vulgar—his melancholic nobility of soul in a world made petty by politics have all served the purposes of bourgeois criticism's self-recognition. In erasing the alterity of this other world it has sought to discover there the same preoccupations and structures as those which govern its own discourse. Politically liberal versions of this unconscious and ideologically loaded modernization of the pre-revolutionary sovereignty, articulating what is either a mild criticism or simply the inheritance of a soured Cartesianism, have even discovered in the prince—fully fledged—that alienated modern individual dejected in the marketplace of inauthentic values. Each has found it necessary to discover in him one recension or another of the subjectivity which defines the modern soul. But in so doing they have necessarily overstated the fullness of the consciousness actually dramatized by the text. The lack of closure in its relentless scepticism, its relativizing, unstable discourse, have been blocked and frozen in order to provide the fixity necessary to recuperate it to a conception of essential subjectivity *fully realized.* In place of the text's pattern of offer and refusal of this interiority, strung out along the chain of Hamlet's rich but fleeting language, a single "problem," or knot of problems, is diagnosed, and is then said to denote him truly. The startling effect has been to reproduce the text as the great tragedy of . . . *bourgeois* culture.

But the point is not to supply this absence, to make whole what is lacking, but to aggravate its historical significance. *Hamlet* is a contradictory, transitional text, and one not yet fully assimilated into the discursive order which has claimed it: the promise of essential subjectivity remains unfulfilled. From its point of vantage on the threshold of the modern but not yet within it, the text scandalously reveals the emptiness at the heart of that bourgeois trope. Rather than the plenitude of an individual presence, the text dramatizes its impossibility. Not only is the myth by which the autonomous individual is made the undetermined unit of being, in contrast to an inert social world, alien to this dramatic regime, but even when, in a later settlement, the philosophical legislation and discursive underpinning necessary to support the device have been provided, it will achieve a success whose stability, as the example of Pepys shows, is at best fragile. When it does emerge in the discourse of a Descartes or a Pepys, in a different kind of writing from that of the Jacobean spectacle as its substantial and founding mode, it will immediately begin to be naturalized as the figure under which the social conditions of another sovereignty will be lived. Itself socially constructed none the less, and not in any event identical with those, or any, social conditions themselves—for in dividing the subject from the outer world it enacts an imaginary desocialization of subjectivity—it will take up its place as the central figure in which bourgeois society will be experienced in interiority and subjection. Its dramatic impossibility in *Hamlet* is, therefore, the more critically valuable for those like ourselves who must still live it out. Rather than a gap to be filled, the vacuity in Hamlet is a "failure" to be celebrated against the more systematically vacuous dominion of the order of subjectivity it both signals and resists.

But if Hamlet's promised but unfulfilled interiority in its sharpest form is unacceptable to bourgeois ideology because it is not sufficiently fixated, it is equally intolerable to the plenum which surrounds him because it has already moved too far in that direction. The text, too, effects its own closure of the fissure that the prince opens in its fabric, and averts the challenge to its order which the prince represents. This is why it mobilizes so many simulacra of him. Fortinbras, Laertes, even the semi-mythical Pyrrhus of the First Player's speech—whose sword also hesitates above the head of a king—are each interference repetitions of Hamlet by which the text disperses across its surface (in a distribution fitted to the spatial dimension of the spectacle) other, external versions of the prince, in order to fend off the insistence of his unique essentiality. And it is why, in order that the play may end, a second Hamlet must be introduced. For rather than the maturation or development of "character" that we have been taught to look for in Shakespeare, there is a quasi-Brechtian discretion between the figure who is deported to England and the figure who returns having suffered a sea change. The agnostic melancholic is replaced by the man of action who does battle with the pirates, and who devises an effective stratagem against the king's agents which he sardonically reports to Horatio:

> HORATIO. So Guildenstern and Rosencrantz go to't.
> HAMLET. Why, man, they did make love to this employment.
> (V.ii.56–57)

The Hamlet who delays (and whose delaying is but the linear deployment of the "vertical" absence within) is replaced by one who simply waits, for whom "it will be short, the interim is mine" (V.ii.74): and who is soon dead; by one whose first appearance, at Ophelia's graveside, is signalled by the fact that the riddling, sliding language of the first Hamlet has now migrated to the mouth of the gravedigger from whom, ironically, the second must now try to elicit simple answers to simple questions; and, finally, by one who goes to his death inserted into the traditional Christian values—the "special providence in the fall of a sparrow" (V.ii.217–18) and the "divinity that shapes our ends, / Rough-hew them how we will (V.ii.10–11) — that were so profoundly questioned by the figure he supplants. By these devices, arbitrarily and theatrically secured, the challenge of Hamlet's incipient modernity is extinguished — for a time — and the prince recuperated to the order of the spectacle which his opacity had troubled.

Chronology

1564	William Shakespeare born at Stratford-on-Avon to John Shakespeare, a butcher, and Mary Arden. He is baptized on April 26.
1582	Marries Anne Hathaway in November.
1583	Daughter Susanna born, baptized on May 26.
1585	Twins Hamnet and Judith born, baptized on February 2.
1588–89	First plays are performed in London.
1588–90	Sometime during these years, Shakespeare goes to London, without family.
1590–92	*The Comedy of Errors,* the three parts of *Henry VI.*
1593–94	Publication of *Venus and Adonis* and *The Rape of Lucrece,* both dedicated to the Earl of Southampton. Shakespeare becomes a sharer in the Lord Chamberlain's company of actors. *The Taming of the Shrew, Two Gentlemen of Verona, Richard III.*
1595–97	*Romeo and Juliet, Richard II, King John, A Midsummer Night's Dream, Love's Labor's Lost.*
1596	Son Hamnet dies. Grant of arms to father.
1597	*The Merchant of Venice, Henry IV* Part I. Purchases New Place in Stratford.
1598–1600	*Henry IV* Part II, *As You Like It, Much Ado About Nothing, Twelfth Night, The Merry Wives of Windsor, Henry V, Julius Caesar.* Moves his company to the new Globe Theatre.
1601	*Hamlet.* Shakespeare's father dies, buried on September 8.
1603	Death of Queen Elizabeth; James VI of Scotland becomes James I of England; Shakespeare's company becomes the King's Men.
1603–04	*All's Well That Ends Well, Measure for Measure, Othello.*
1605–06	*King Lear, Macbeth.*
1607	Marriage of daughter Susanna on June 5.
1607–08	*Timon of Athens, Antony and Cleopatra, Pericles.*
1608	Death of Shakespeare's mother. Buried on September 9.

1609   *Cymbeline,* publication of sonnets. Shakespeare's company purchases Blackfriars Theatre.

1610–11   *The Winter's Tale, The Tempest.* Shakespeare retires to Stratford.

1616   Marriage of daughter Judith on February 10. William Shakespeare dies at Stratford on April 23.

1623   Publication of the Folio edition of Shakespeare's plays.

Contributors

HAROLD BLOOM, Sterling Professor of the Humanities at Yale University, is the author of *The Anxiety of Influence, Poetry and Repression,* and many other volumes of literary criticism. His forthcoming study, *Freud: Transference and Authority,* attempts a full-scale reading of all of Freud's major writings. A MacArthur Prize Fellow, he is general editor of five series of literary criticism published by Chelsea House.

HAROLD GODDARD was head of the English Department at Swarthmore College from 1909 to 1946. He is remembered not only for *The Meaning of Shakespeare,* but also for his writings upon American Transcendentalism.

HARRY LEVIN is Irving Babbitt Professor of Comparative Literature, Emeritus, at Harvard University. His books include *The Gates of Horn, The Overreacher: A Study of Christopher Marlowe* and *Shakespeare and the Revolution of the Times.*

RUTH NEVO is Professor of English at Hebrew University at Jerusalem. She is the author of *The Dial of Virtue* and *Comic Transformations in Shakespeare.*

LAWRENCE DANSON is Professor of English at Princeton University. He is the author of *The Harmonies of "The Merchant of Venice."*

RICHARD A. LANHAM is Professor of English at the University of California, Los Angeles. His other books include *"Tristram Shandy": The Games of Pleasure* and *Literacy and the Survival of Humanism.*

HOWARD FELPERIN is Robert Wallace Professor of Post-Medieval Literature at the University of Melbourne. He is the author of *Shakespearean Romance* and *Shakespearean Representation.*

MARK ROSE is Professor of English at the University of California, Santa Barbara. His books include *Heroic Love: Studies in Sidney & Spenser* and *Shakespearean Design.*

FRANCIS BARKER is Lecturer in Literature at the University of Essex, England. He is an editor of several volumes on the sociology of literature.

Bibliography

Allman, Eileen J. *Player-King and Adversary.* Baton Rouge and London: Louisiana State University Press, 1980.

Brown, John Russell, and Bernard Harris, eds. *Hamlet.* London: Edward Arnold (Publishers) Ltd., 1963.

Charney, Maurice. *Style in "Hamlet."* Princeton: Princeton University Press, 1969.

Cox, Lee Sheridan. *Figurative Design in "Hamlet": The Significance of the Dumb Show.* Columbus: Ohio State University Press, 1973.

Dillon, Janette. *Shakespeare and the Solitary Man.* London and Basingstoke: Macmillan Press, 1981.

Eliot, T. S. *Selected Essays,* new edition. New York: Harcourt Brace, 1950.

Fergusson, Francis. *The Idea of a Theater.* Princeton: Princeton University Press, 1965.

Fisch, Harold. *"Hamlet" and the Word.* New York: Frederick Ungar Publishing Co., 1971.

Flatter, Richard. *Hamlet's Father.* London: William Heinemann, Ltd., 1949.

Gottschalk, Paul. *The Meanings of "Hamlet."* Albuquerque: University of New Mexico Press, 1972.

Holland, Norman N. *Psychoanalysis and Shakespeare.* New York: McGraw-Hill, 1966.

Jones, Ernest. *Hamlet and Oedipus.* New York: W. W. Norton & Company, Inc. 1949.

Joyce, James. *Ulysses.* New York: Random House, Inc., 1961.

King, Walter N. *Hamlet's Search for Meaning.* Athens: University of Georgia Press, 1982.

Knight, George Wilson. *The Wheel of Fire.* London: Methuen & Co., Ltd., 1949.

Knights, L. C. *An Approach to "Hamlet."* Stanford: Stanford University Press, 1961.

Lacan, Jacques. "Desire and the Interpretation of Desire in 'Hamlet.'" Translated by James Hulbert. *Yale French Studies* 55–56 (1977).

Lewis, C. S. "Hamlet: The Prince or the Poem?" *Proceedings of the British Academy* 28 (1942): 139–54.

Long, Michael. *The Unnatural Scene.* London: Methuen & Co., Ltd., 1976.

Mack, Maynard, Jr. *Killing the King: Three Studies in Shakespeare's Tragic Structure.* New Haven and London: Yale University Press, 1973.

Nuttal, A. D. *A New Mimesis: Shakespeare and the Representation of Reality.* London: Methuen & Co., Ltd., 1983.

Prosser, Eleanor. *Hamlet and Revenge.* Stanford: Stanford University Press, 1971.

Robertson, J. M. *The Problem of "Hamlet."* London: George Allen & Unwin, Ltd., 1919.

Rose, Mark. *Shakespearean Design.* Cambridge: The Belknap Press, 1972.

Schwartz, Murray M., and Coppelia Kahn, eds. *Representing Shakespeare.* Baltimore and London: The Johns Hopkins University Press, 1980.

Siemon, James R. *Shakespearean Iconoclasm.* Berkeley and Los Angeles: University of California Press, 1985.

Waldock, A. J. A. *"Hamlet": A Study in Critical Method.* Cambridge: Cambridge University Press, 1931.

Wilson, John Dover. *What Happens in "Hamlet."* Cambridge: Cambridge University Press, 1935.

Acknowledgments

"Hamlet: His Own Falstaff" (originally entitled "Hamlet") by Harold Goddard from *The Meaning of Shakespeare* by Harold Goddard, © 1951 by The University of Chicago. Reprinted by permission of The University of Chicago Press.

"An Explication of the Player's Speech" by Harry Levin from *The Question of Hamlet* by Harry Levin, © 1959 by Oxford University Press, Inc. Reprinted by permission.

"Acts III and IV: Problems of Text and Staging" (originally entitled "Hamlet") by Ruth Nevo from *Tragic Form in Shakespeare* by Ruth Nevo, © 1972 by Princeton University Press. Reprinted by permission.

"Tragic Alphabet" (originally entitled "Hamlet") by Lawrence Danson from *Tragic Alphabet: Shakespeare's Drama of Language* by Lawrence Danson, © 1974 by Yale University. Reprinted by permission of Yale University Press.

"Superposed Plays" (originally entitled "Superposed Plays: *Hamlet*") by Richard A. Lanham from *The Motives of Eloquence: Literary Rhetoric in the Renaissance* by Richard A. Lanham, © 1976 by Yale University. Reprinted by permission of Yale University Press.

"O'erdoing Termagant" (originally entitled "O'erdoing Termagant: An Approach to Shakespearean Mimesis") by Howard Felperin from *The Yale Review* 63, no. 3 (Spring 1974), © 1974 by Yale University. Reprinted by permission of *The Yale Review*.

"Reforming the Role" (originally entitled "Hamlet") by Mark Rose from *Homer to Brecht: The European Epic and Dramatic Traditions,* edited by Michael Seidel and Edward Mendelson, © 1977 by Yale University. Reprinted by permission of Yale University Press.

"Pre-Pepysian Theatre: A Challenged Spectacle" (originally entitled "A Challenged Spectacle") by Francis Barker from *The Tremulous Private Body: Essays on Subjection* by Francis Barker, © 1984 by Francis Barker. Reprinted by permission of Methuen & Co., Ltd.

Index